TRUMP
STRATEGIES
FOR
REAL ESTATE

TRUMP STRATEGIES FOR REAL ESTATE

Billionaire Lessons for the Small Investor

GEORGE H. ROSS

with

Andrew James McLean

WILEY

JOHN WILEY & SONS, INC.

Published by John Wiley & Sons, Inc., Hoboken, New Jersey.
Published simultaneously in Canada.

For general information on our other products and services please contact our Customer
Care Department within the United States at (800) 762-2974, outside the United States
at (317) 572-3993 or fax (317) 572-4002.

Wiley also publishes its books in a variety of electronic formats. Some content that
appears in print may not be available in electronic books. For more information about
Wiley products, visit our web site at www.wiley.com.

Library of Congress Cataloging-in-Publication Data:

Ross, George H., 1928–
   Trump strategies for real estate : billionaire lessons for the small
investor / George H. Ross with Andrew James McLean.
      p. cm.
   Includes bibliographical references and index.
   ISBN 0-471-71835-1 (cloth)
   1. Real estate investment.   2. Real estate development.   3. Real estate
investment—United States—Case studies.   4. Real estate
development—United States—Case studies.   5. Trump, Donald, 1946–   I.
Title: Billionaire lessons for the small investor.   II. McLean, Andrew
James.   III. Title.
   HD1382.5.R67 2005
   332.63'24—dc22

                                                                      2005000053

Printed in the United States of America.

10 9 8 7 6 5 4 3 2 1

This book is dedicated to my wonderful wife, Billie
the solid foundation on which the happiness and success
in my life was built.

CONTENTS

CONTENTS

FOREWORD

by

Donald Trump

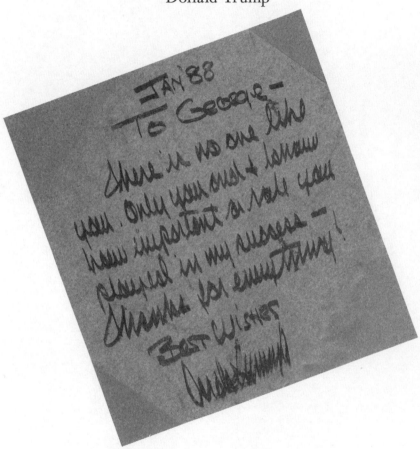

(In the author's copy of *The Art of the Deal*)

To George—

There is no one like you. Only you and I know how important a role you played in my success—Thanks for everything!

Best wishes,
Donald Trump

PREFACE

I'VE SPENT 50 YEARS as a lawyer, business advisor, and deal negotiator for real estate tycoons at the top of the world's toughest real
estate market—New York City. I've represented or negotiated with
great real estate minds like Harry Helmsley, Sam LeFrak, Bill Zeckendorf, and Donald Trump. It's been my good fortune to spend many
of the best years of my career as Donald's right-hand man.

These days most people know me best from the TV show, *The
Apprentice*, where Carolyn Kepcher and I help Donald make tough
decisions about whom to fire and whom to keep. The show has been
fun, but most of my work for Donald over the past 25 years has been
in the world of real estate. I have been an advisor, negotiator, and
lawyer on many of his biggest and most successful real estate investments, including the acquisition and renovation of the GM building,
Trump Tower on 5th Avenue, the Grand Hyatt Hotel, and my personal favorite, 40 Wall Street.

Throughout my career, I have had the opportunity to acquire a
great deal of knowledge and experience in real estate investing,
which I hope to pass on to you in this book. For example, during a
10-year period from 1956 to 1966 when Sol Goldman and Alex
DiLorenzo Jr. became two of the biggest property owners in New
York, I personally bought 702 individual properties on their behalf. I
have been intimately involved in many of New York City's most
spectacular projects, such as the Chrysler Building and the St. Regis

Hotel, which I helped one of my clients buy. I've also had the opportunity to watch Donald Trump in action as he made some of the greatest real estate investments in history.

This book explains the strategies Donald Trump used to make his real estate fortune, and how small investors can apply them to investments of any size, right down to a one-family rental property. I describe how Trump implements some of his signature strategies such as creating luxury, perceived value, exclusivity, and attention to detail, which all come together to maximize the value of his investments. (This is why his properties earn far more money, square foot for square foot, than his competitors'.)

A number of the chapters focus on a particular real estate investment that I was directly involved in negotiating or advising Trump on. Using this example, I draw out the lessons and explain how the same strategies that Trump used to make huge profits on his deals can work for you—the small investor. Although Trump does things on a grand scale and his target market is usually an elite, luxury customer, Trump's basic real estate strategies will be of interest to:

- Anyone who is interested in owning or developing real estate
- Anyone unsure of how to negotiate a real estate transaction
- Anyone who is in real estate on a small scale but would like to do more
- Anyone interested in learning how Donald Trump does his magic

This is the first book on Trump's strategies for the real estate investor. Although it has a lot of nuts-and-bolts guidance and investing principles, the book alone will not make you a great investor. As I tell the students who take my negotiation course at New York University, "There's no way in 15 hours that I can make you an excellent negotiator. It is impossible! All I want to do is open your mind to the possibilities and the power of negotiating, and some basic techniques. Then, when you run into a specific situation you can go back to your notes, and say, how did George handle this? Or, what did he suggest?" You already have some ideas about real estate, but I've learned many things in my 25 years working with Trump and 50 years in the real estate business, that I'd like to pass along to you. If I am successful, this book will help you negotiate far better deals, arrange better financing, make better investments, and earn significantly more money in real estate.

I recall the day I first met Donald Trump in 1974. He entered my office at the law firm of Dreyer and Traub beaming with enthusiasm about a project he wanted to do with the old Commodore Hotel on 42d Street in New York City. He was just 27 years old at the time, and I was a senior partner known for completing complex deals, but I agreed to see him out of courtesy because I represented his father, Fred Trump. Fred had spoken enthusiastically about Donald's promise as a future star in the real estate world.

Donald laid out his incredibly complex plan for buying the huge, dumpy, rundown hotel next to Grand Central Station and turning it into a first-class, state-of-the-art business hotel. I told him it was a brilliant idea, but there was no way it would ever work, given the number of powerful people and governmental agencies he would have to convince to grant him major concessions. Nevertheless, if he was willing to pay the legal fees, I was willing to help him take a shot at it. We spent the next two years negotiating with railroad executives, city and state officials, lenders, and Hyatt executives making the deal happen. During those tumultuous two years, Donald and I developed a great working relationship and mutual respect. When he miraculously pulled off the deal, I was so sure he would be a huge success in real estate that I became his closest advisor and lawyer.

How My Career Started

When I was young, growing up in Brooklyn, New York, I planned to go to MIT to be an engineer, but my father died suddenly when I was 16 and that plan died with him. At 17 I enlisted in the U.S. Army because they offered to send me to college. When I went on active duty, I was trained as a cryptanalyst (a code breaker) and spent most of my short army career in Washington, DC. The analytical skills, patience, and tenacity I learned as a code breaker helped me when I was faced with seemingly unresolvable real estate problems.

With the help of the GI Bill, I obtained my BA degree at Brooklyn College and entered Brooklyn Law School. Working three jobs concurrently and with the support of my working wife, I graduated and was admitted to the New York Bar in 1953.

While looking for a job, I saw an ad in the *Law Journal* for a law clerk. As luck would have it, the person who answered the phone was Bill, a friend from law school. He was working for Dreyer and Traub, a well-known real estate law firm. Bill said, "You don't want this job. You'll be nothing but a messenger and it only pays $25 a week." But I took it anyway! That was the inauspicious beginning of my legal career.

Although Dreyer and Traub was a law firm dealing primarily with real estate matters, they handled litigation as a courtesy for their clients, and Bill and I worked in the litigation department. Several months later there was an opening upstairs in the real estate acquisition and leasing practice, the place where real money was made. It was an excellent opportunity for advancement and Bill was slotted for the job. I was to take his spot in litigation. But before he could start, he was drafted into the army and recommended me for the real estate position. Once upstairs, I had the good fortune to apprentice to Murray Felton, a very tough taskmaster. He was so demanding that if I put a comma in the wrong place, I would hear about it for days. But Felton was a superb technician and highly regarded in the world of real estate attorneys. I knew that working with him was a great opportunity to learn the intricacies of real estate law from a perfectionist. So I soaked up every bit of helpful information I could from him. I became adept at drafting leases, real estate documents, and participating in all types of transactions. My prior litigation experience added to the perception that I was a competent, though young, real estate attorney.

LEARNING THE REAL ESTATE BUSINESS

In 1955, one of my clients asked me to draft a commercial lease for him even though he was to be the tenant. Usually, the landlord's attorney drafts the lease, but in this case the landlord told my client to have his lawyer prepare the lease. So I drew up the lease and inserted a provision stating that the tenant didn't have to pay any rent before the landlord made a certain elevator operational. My client moved in and, as it turned out, the elevator inspector for New York City refused to accept the elevator repairs the landlord made, insisting that only a brand new elevator would get his approval. The elevator stayed out of operation for a very long time, but throughout that period my client was still able to carry out his normal business operations.

The owners, Sol Goldman and Alex DiLorenzo Jr. had a "tenant in possession" utilizing the premises for its normal business operations, but because of that clause in the lease, the tenant was not paying them any rent! Although the landlords were very unhappy they were helpless.

In the mid-1950s, Goldman and DiLorenzo, who were both multimillionaires, had decided to invest in real estate on a huge scale. I had decided to leave Dreyer and Traub because I had been told that there was no possibility for me to become a partner in the firm. I happened to mention my impending departure to Sol Goldman and he called me a few days later and said, "George, Alex and I would like you to be our counsel." I said, "Why me?" He said, "Well, we already paid $90,000 in the form of lost rent just for the privilege of knowing you! We'll make it worth your while if you say yes." I accepted their offer.

EVERY PROBLEM HAS A PRICE TAG

Very quickly I learned something that every real estate investor should understand: There is a huge difference between the legal aspects of real estate and the business of investing in real estate. I had to restructure my whole way of thinking. Whenever I discovered a legal problem with a real estate deal, Goldman would say, "Is it serious enough to blow the deal?" If I said, "No." Then he would say, "How much can I get off the price for the problem?" Most lawyers simply advise their clients not to do a deal if they find legal problems; lawyers cannot or will not make business recommendations for their clients. Goldman forced me to think like a businessman, not just a lawyer, and realize that almost every problem has a price tag. He forced me to look at legal problems strictly as a way of improving the deal. He'd say, "What can I get if I overlook this problem?" To find that answer, I had to dig into the problem.

For example, Goldman and DiLorenzo contracted to buy Harborside Terminal in Jersey City, New Jersey, from the railroad that owned it. The property consisted of a huge cold storage warehouse of almost two million square feet abutting the Hudson River, right across the river from downtown Manhattan. The purchase price seemed reasonable even though it was to be an all-cash deal. However, the title report contained an exception for possible claims of the State of New Jersey to a strip of land that the warehouse straddled. It became clear to me why the railroad was having difficulty finding a buyer. No lawyer would let a client buy the property with such a defect and certainly no bank would place a mortgage on it. The problem related to land under water that was filled in sometime in the 1800s. A law was passed stipulating that if the land under water was filled in by the adjoining landowner before 1849, the landowner had good title to it. If it was filled in after 1849, the State of New Jersey owned it. I couldn't prove when it was filled in and who filled it nor could the State of New Jersey.

I told Sol we should get a price reduction and also convince the railroad to take back a long-term purchase money mortgage at a low interest rate since no lender would make any loan because of the title defect. The railroad agreed to reduce the purchase price by $400,000 and to take a sizable mortgage, so we closed the deal. Several years went by but the title impediment still stuck in my craw. I was certain that the State of New Jersey must have encountered the same problem in the past since much of the land abutting the Hudson River was filled-in land. I contacted the State and learned that they were aware of the problem and rather than sit with a dubious claim they had passed a statute giving the State the right to give up its claim in exchange for the value of their interest in the disputed land. Following the procedure outlined in the statute, we paid a minimal amount and received a quitclaim deed to the land in dispute from the State of New Jersey. As a result, the property appreciated in value so much that a bank made a first mortgage loan in an amount exceeding the total purchase price paid by Goldman and DiLorenzo.

From 1956 to 1966 Goldman and DiLorenzo *were* New York real estate. When I arrived at Goldman and DiLorenzo in 1956, they owned 18 properties; when I left in 1966, they owned 720. I negotiated and handled almost all of these purchases by myself with very little supervision from them. We were buying Manhattan ground leases by the dozen, warehouses in New York harbor, and multimillion-dollar office buildings. We were dealing in big numbers, and much of it was done with cash. Many times I walked into a closing on a property with a certified check for millions of dollars in my wallet. I was also given a standing million dollar deposit by Goldman and DiLorenzo with which to negotiate. Goldman and DiLorenzo would tell me what type of deal they wanted and my job was to make it happen. They were not anxious buyers, so if I didn't think the deal met their terms, I would kill it and go on to the next one. That's what enabled them to acquire so much real estate so quickly. During that 10-year period, I bought the Chrysler Building, the St. Regis Hotel, the land under the Plaza Hotel, Harborside Terminal in Jersey City, and numerous ground leases on their behalf. (A *ground lease* is a long-term lease for land on which a building sits, and gives the tenant all the rights and obligations of operation and ownership except title to the land.)

Goldman and DiLorenzo's appetite for real estate was voracious. They had excellent financing connections which enabled me to close transactions quickly. As their lone lawyer and business representative, I had almost unlimited authority to negotiate but not to increase the purchase price. I negotiated with Harry Helmsley, Bill Zeckendorf, and Morris Karp to name a few. These were all the big names in New York real estate at that particular time—pretty heady stuff for a 30-year-old lawyer.

For the first few years I worked for Goldman and DiLorenzo, I was in way over my head. At Dreyer and Traub, I was handling closings on single-family homes in New Jersey. I had never done a contract and closing on any office building of any size. Now I was thrust into an arena involving the purchase and operation of huge office buildings. I really had no prior training or experience. Yet everyone thought, because I was so young and represented these millionaires in huge transactions, I must be brilliant so they treated me as an equal. I knew how green I was, but I wasn't going to dispute their assessment of me! I learned as fast as I could from everyone I came in contact with, including all the people on the other side—the lawyers and other professionals and the real estate moguls themselves. I concentrated on what they did, how they did it, how they acted and reacted in certain situations, and anything else that would fill the void of my ineptitude. I was like a sponge absorbing every bit of information I could. Before long my crash course in real estate paid off and I began to give my clients well-reasoned opinions as to which deals were good and which were not and what price to pay. This gave me a unique combination of talents. Most lawyers don't know the business of real estate, and therefore, they are not equipped to make business decisions. They are ready to render advice on any legal issue, but leave the business decisions to their client.

Radio Days

Any good lawyer will make lots of money while practicing law, but since lawyering is a service business, the income stops when you step down. I recognized the need to invest in some enterprise that would be of value in my later years. In 1966, my brother-in-law, Martin Beck, was leaving the Katz Agency, a big name in the business of selling radio time. He suggested that we look for investment opportunities together. He thought radio broadcasting on Long Island would be profitable. I told him, "I don't know anything about the radio business." He said, "I know all about radio but I don't know how to raise the capital necessary for a venture." I told him, "You find and run the stations and I'll find the money to make it happen." In 1966, we formed Beck-Ross Communications Corporation and bought our first radio station in Long Island, WGLI, for approximately $450,000. Marty knew how to make money in radio broadcasting. Using the profits from WGLI and by expanding our financial contacts, we embarked on a plan of expansion. FM broadcasting was in its infancy but the superiority of the sound made it an attractive prospect. We purchased several other stations—both AM and FM—increased their market share, and then sold them at huge profits. In 1986, Marty and I bought out all of our investors for 25 times their original investment. In 1987, we were faced with a decision that many investors confront at some time, to expand the business or sell out to someone who would. We chose to take a substantial profit and leave the expansion to the buyer.

But the radio business was only a sideline to my law career. In 1966, after 10 years with Goldman and DiLorenzo, my reputation had grown to the point where I could have received a partnership with any quality law firm with a real estate department. I opted to return as a partner to my old firm, Dreyer and Traub, where I was being accepted as a senior partner. I realized that since only two young attorneys had become new partners in the past 10 years and the old partners were reaching retirement, it would be my firm within a few years. That's exactly what happened. By the early 1970s, I became one of four senior partners running one of the best real estate law firms in New York with as many as 120 lawyers. I led that firm for more than 20 years.

Eventually, I got tired of dealing with partnership politics, gave up the active practice of law, got a severance package, and joined the Edward S. Gordon Company where my role for the next 10 years was to supply real estate expertise to major clients like United Technologies, IBM, the *New York Times*, and AT&T.

HOW I CAME TO WORK FOR DONALD TRUMP

Although I left the active practice of law in 1987, I remained friendly with Donald Trump, and though I had worked with him on many of his most successful projects, I was no longer his lawyer. When the New York City real estate market tanked in 1990, Trump hit the rocks. It was not due to a lack of business acumen; rather, his phenomenal success had created an air of invincibility. Because he had been so incredibly successful, he began to think that any business he touched would turn to gold.

The banks would throw money at him. If he asked to borrow $60 million for a building, they gave him $80 million. When the bottom fell out of the New York City real estate market, he was vastly overextended and was over $990 million in debt. He owed so much money that the lenders knew if they forced him into bankruptcy it would have a disastrous effect on the real estate market. They had many bad loans that they didn't want to write off. So they came up with a plan that would enable him to work his way back by agreeing to accept a substantial reduction if the loans were repaid by a certain future date.

Even though I was no longer a member of a law firm, I wanted to help. I told Donald that if he ever needed legal advice or counsel while he was in trouble, I would be happy to do it for him without charge. He was impressed and asked me why I would do that. I said, "Donald, I think a lawyer has a responsibility to represent a client when he's down, not only when he's on top. I'm here if you need me." Trump never accepted my offer because it's not his style to get something for nothing. But I'm sure he appreciated the gesture. My philosophy has since paid off in spades—with Donald Trump, loyalty goes a long way.

In the mid-1990s, Donald had two deals going, the new Nike Building adjoining Trump Tower and 40 Wall Street. Both were plagued with problems because of the lawyers involved, and very little was getting accomplished. Donald knows when to use delay tactics, but he also hates deals that drag on and on. So he hired me to eliminate the roadblocks and get those deals done. While I was working on them, I told Donald that I was bored with my life at Gordon and was planning to retire. He asked me to join the Trump Organization on a full-time basis. He said, "I've got a lot of great things going and you'll have fun." We quickly agreed on terms (I only work four days a week) and 10 years later, I'm still an important part of the Trump team.

My title is Senior Executive Vice President and Senior Counsel for the Trump Organization and my primary function is to give Donald Trump business and legal advice. I offer my opinion as to the feasibility of his proposed projects, which he is free to accept or reject. He likes to bounce things off me before reaching his own decision. He knows that I will call it like I see it and give him an unbiased opinion. I'm currently responsible for developing many foreign investments for Donald and supervising the leasing and operation of 40 Wall Street and Trump Tower.

Additionally, I teach a course at New York University on negotiation. Negotiation is a subject that I have made a study of throughout my career, because it is such a critical part of real estate success. I could easily fill a book on this subject. For a discussion of some of the principles and techniques, used by Trump, that I think are most valuable, see Chapters 3 and 4.

Trump has been a great man to work for. In 10 years, he has never once asked me where I'm going or what I'm doing. That's the kind of trust we have. When he gave me responsibility for 40 Wall Street, I took the building from where it was—a one-million-square-foot nearly vacant structure he purchased for $1 million—to where it is now—a thriving office building worth in excess of $350 million. After 40 Wall Street had been rented and had become extremely profitable for Trump, I said to him, "I think I'm entitled to a bonus for 40 Wall Street." Trump's reply was, "How much do you think you're entitled to?" I gave him a figure. He said, "You've got it." It's this kind of recognition that makes it a pleasure to work for him.

Fred Trump once said to Donald when he needed a lawyer, "You would be hard-pressed to find a wiser, more loyal, or a better advisor and lawyer than George Ross." I'm delighted Donald took that advice and gave me the opportunity to work with a true real estate genius. Now I hope to pass on to you some of the powerful investing strategies I've learned from some of the greatest real estate minds in the business.

ACKNOWLEDGMENTS

My gratitude to Donald J. Trump for becoming such an important part of my life as a friend and for giving me the unique opportunity throughout my career to help turn his visions of spectacular projects into realities.

1

SELL YOURSELF LIKE TRUMP

Five Personal Qualities You Need to Succeed in Real Estate

KEY POINTS

- Use your enthusiasm for the project to inspire others.
- Build relationships with everyone involved in a deal.
- Showmanship is a real estate strategy.
- Be better prepared than anyone else.
- Be tenacious.

Grand Hyatt

DONALD TRUMP BECAME a billionaire in real estate by making a series of incredibly creative and successful investments in New York City properties. He is now the largest real estate developer in New York and is widely acknowledged to be one of the most brilliant real estate investing minds anywhere. For example, in the early 1980s, with the building of Trump Tower on 5th Avenue, he single-handedly created the market for high-end luxury residences in New York City. He continued with a string of successes and in 2003, 9 of the 10 highest selling apartments were in Trump buildings—apartments that sold for millions of dollars each.

What can the small real estate investor learn from a billionaire developer like Trump? After advising Trump on many of his biggest investments over 25 years, I'm convinced that small investors can successfully use many of the same principles that earn him millions. It's not the scale of your real estate investment project that counts. Whether you are investing in a single-family rental, a four-unit rental, or a multimillion-dollar office building makes no difference to the financial success of your particular project, what's important are the real estate investing strategies used to acquire and develop the property, and how you design and market the property to buyers or tenants. Many of the same basic principles that work for one of Trump's $300-million skyscrapers work just as well for smaller properties. Anyone interested in investing in real estate can benefit from a study of Trump's real estate investor strategies.

For example, you can't make big real estate investments—or really profitable small investments—without projecting certain personal qualities that inspire confidence in others, and make them want to help you or to see things your way. The key personal qualities you need are enthusiasm, relationship-building skills, showmanship, preparation, and tenacity. Donald Trump has these qualities in spades as he demonstrated on his first big real estate deal, the transformation of the dilapidated Commodore Hotel on 42nd Street in New York City into the magnificent Grand Hyatt. Remarkably, Trump used very little of his own money in this transaction, yet later sold his half interest to Hyatt for $85 million.

   This chapter will describe how these five key personal qualities helped Trump make the Commodore-Hyatt deal work, and how small investors can use these same qualities in their own real estate investments to negotiate better deals, sell properties for more money, and dramatically improve real estate profits.

INVESTING CASE STUDY

TRUMP'S COMMODORE-HYATT PROJECT

This real estate investment was a monster as far as complexity was concerned. It was 1974, New York City was struggling to survive, and Trump decided that this was a great time to buy a huge, dilapidated, nearly empty building on 42nd Street next to Grand Central Station. Like many of the best real estate investors, he looks at problem properties and sees opportunities. Trump's plan was to convert this old building, the Commodore Hotel, into a 1,400-room first-class convention hotel—the largest since the New York Hilton was built 25 years earlier.

   When 27-year-old Donald Trump explained his grandiose idea to me during our first meeting, I told him that based on existing conditions he was chasing an impossible dream that would never happen. I thought the idea was brilliant, but it was totally unrealistic given the economic environment and the huge cast of characters who would have to embrace a set of entirely new concepts for the idea to work. Trump would have to win major financial concessions from:

1. Penn Central, a bankrupt railroad that owned the land on which the Commodore Hotel was built;
2. New York City, which was facing bankruptcy;
3. The State of New York, which had no money to contribute to any venture;
4. A lender who was holding many defaulted loans on New York real estate;
5. A major hotel chain that was not pursuing new facilities in New York City since tourism and occupancy rates were extremely low; and
6. Existing tenants occupying the building.

The deal involved successful negotiation of several treacherous interconnected transactions. If Trump failed to conclude any one of these transactions, it would sink the entire project. Using the five personal qualities outlined in this chapter he had to:

1. Obtain an option to buy the Commodore Hotel from the Penn Central Railroad for $12 million dollars;
2. Convince the representatives of Penn Central Railroad to turn over the $12 million purchase price to New York City, which was owed $15 million in back taxes from the Penn Central;
3. Convince New York City to accept the $12 million to cover $15 million in back taxes and agree to the creation of a long-term lease that would give the city a share of profits in lieu of future real estate taxes;
4. Convince the Urban Development Corporation, a New York State Agency, to accept title to the property, then grant a long-term

lease of the property to Trump and to use its right of eminent domain to obtain possession from existing tenants;

5. Find a major hotel operator willing to participate in the ownership and operation of the new hotel to give credibility to the creation of profits in which New York City would share; and

6. Find a bank willing to lend $80 million to cover all of the costs in-
volved in purchasing and developing the property.

This was as complex as it sounds. Something like this had never
been done before.

To jump ahead to the end of the story, Trump pulled it off,
convincing all these parties to work with him, using his enthusiasm,
relationship-building skills, showmanship, preparation, and tenacity.
In September of 1980, the Grand Hyatt opened—and it was a great
success from day one. The renovated Hyatt helped revitalize the
whole Grand Central Station neighborhood in New York City, which
in turn played a major role in reversing the failing, bankrupt image of
the city in the 1970s. By 1987, gross operating profits at the Hyatt
exceeded $30 million annually. Years later, after recouping his mod-
est cash investment in the property, Trump sold his half interest to
Hyatt for $85 million.

Here's how Donald Trump used critical personal qualities to clinch
that monumental real estate deal. You can use the same qualities in
your own dealings regardless of their size or complexity.

USE YOUR ENTHUSIASM FOR THE
PROJECT TO INSPIRE OTHERS

Enthusiasm is a crucial element of the investment game because your
success depends largely on capturing the imagination and securing

the cooperation of key players—buyers, sellers, lenders, tenants, contractors, and others. If you're not enthusiastic about your real estate investment idea, there's no way you can get someone else to sign on. Remember that people will initially be skeptical of whatever you say. So be like Trump, sell hard. If you can maintain your level of commitment and enthusiasm in the face of initial doubts, you've taken the first step toward getting the support you will need to succeed. Trump knows that *enthusiasm is contagious.*

For example, Trump's enthusiasm for the Commodore-Hyatt project and the way he envisioned it benefiting the entire city of New York were boundless. He communicated his vision over and over to all of the people who were involved in the various governmental agencies, including the mayor's office and the railroad. He argued that this one project could help turn around the entire blighted midtown Manhattan area. They all agreed that it was important to do something about this eyesore, the Commodore, because of its critical location next to Grand Central Station. Trump's enthusiasm convinced them that he was the only person capable of putting all the pieces together. For example, he told the city, "Forget real estate taxes and concentrate on the money you'll earn from room taxes, income taxes paid to the city on the salaries earned by the employees working in the new hotel, and the profits from the hotel operation." (Trump offered to make New York City a partner in the profits.) "Think about how the new construction will bring desperately needed jobs to New York and reestablish New York City as the capital of the world."

Trump's enthusiasm was the catalyst for getting key people, whose support he needed to achieve success, interested in the deal and to getting the city to embrace the idea. He prepared charts and graphics showing the dreary existing conditions of the area, the likelihood of an extended recession in property values leading to further erosion of the city's tax base. He explained, "This is what you've got now but here's what I can do for you." He would then display a dramatic color rendering of the building as it would appear when renovated and sell this as the linchpin of revitalizing the Grand Central area—which in turn was the cornerstone of the reconstruction of the image of New York City. All he initially sought was the city's acknowledgment that this was a great idea coupled with a loose commitment to cooperate in bringing it to fruition, if they got everything they wanted. He never talked numbers with the key players in this deal until after he got an initial expression of interest and support for his plan. He knew that talking numbers too soon would give people a reason to say no to his plan. It's a valuable lesson for you to remember in any real estate investment of yours: Enthusiasm (and focusing initially on the large outlines of a deal rather than the financial details) can overcome many obstacles.

How Small Real Estate Investors Can Use Enthusiasm

The Hotel Commodore conversion was a huge project that took over two years and 23 drafts of a complicated and intensely negotiated ground lease to finish. But no matter what the size or complexity of your real estate project, at various stages of the transaction you'll need to convince other people to help you, and do what you want them to do. This takes enthusiasm and perseverance. Share with the seller, your lenders, contractors, and others what you envision for the property you want to buy or renovate. Tell a great story about how you found it, what your inspiration was, and the difficulties you have already overcome. Play up what you see as its best or most unique features. Trump knows that people like to be excited. You just have to find creative ways to excite them.

If you're not enthusiastic, the people you're trying to convince to lend you money, sell you a property, or invest in your partnership are not going to stick their necks out. But if you can tell a great story about your investment idea, if you are articulate and enthusiastic about the opportunity you are offering others, you are on your way to developing the requisite rapport with buyers, sellers, lenders, or other decision makers.

Build Relationships with
Everyone Involved in a Deal

The success of any real estate investment or any business deal, for that matter, is not strictly a matter of dollars-and-cents. A lot of it comes down to personal relationships—your ability to forge strong cooperative relationships with all parties, whether they are directly or even tangentially involved. Trump does this by taking the time necessary to gain insight into the people he is dealing with—who they are, what they do, how they do business, who are their family members or friends, and if appropriate, what their hobbies are. If you can establish a rapport and a feeling of mutual trust it invariably makes for an easier negotiation and a faster, more amicable conclusion to any problems that arise. The principle here is, "No one intends to buy a bucket of trust but they will pay for it if it's delivered." Give people reasons to trust you by building a relationship with them, and you will be laying the foundation for long-term real estate investing success.

The reason you have to build relationships, especially at the beginning of a real estate transaction, is that people are naturally suspicious of others. Until you have built up a level of trust, it is likely that what you say will be somewhat discounted.

One way to build a good relationship is to assume that the present transaction you're working on is only the beginning of negotiating many deals with your counterparts. Work hard to create the impression of being "a nice person to deal with." Some of Trump's best deals were the result of recommendations from adversaries with whom he had past dealings. Leaving pleasant memories is the best personal advertisement in any real estate transaction.

Here's a great example of Trump's relationship-building skill in action from the Commodore-Hyatt deal. Trump had never met Victor Palmieri, an executive with Penn Central Railroad, which owned the Commodore Hotel, but Trump knew Palmieri would have to play a key role if Trump's idea were to become reality. With full confidence in his project and his salesmanship, Donald Trump called Palmieri, introduced himself, and said, "Give me 15 minutes of your time and we can reverse the decline of the City of New York and increase the value of your Penn Central holdings." In the meeting, Trump got Palmieri's attention and a solid working relationship was created. Without Trump building a strong cooperative relationship with Victor Palmieri, the decision maker for Penn Central, he would have never had the opportunity to purchase the Commodore from Penn Central, let alone get Palmieri's help in pressuring the city for its cooperation, which became critical later on.

Small investors tend to think that they have no basis for building a personal relationship, and therefore no negotiating power. Negative thoughts create their own problems. You may be dealing with someone who's much more successful, or who works for a large, impersonal bank. You may think they can't (or won't) relate to you, but that's not true. You can relate to each other as human beings. Look for anything at all you may have in common.

If you're going into a meeting with someone, learn as much about them beforehand as you can. Ask someone else about them, find out what they know. If you're going to meet with an owner of a rental property, speak to one of his tenants beforehand. Ask questions, such as, Is it a good property? What do you think about the landlord?

Now you have information that may help you establish rapport with the owner, and probably some ammunition that will be useful when you enter into negotiations.

Showmanship Is a Real Estate Strategy

Once you have conviction about how your real estate investment can benefit not just you but the other people whose help you need, and you've started to build relationships, the next step is to find concrete ways to communicate your vision to your potential real estate partners. Anyone who is involved with a real estate transaction, especially a fixer-upper project or new construction, has undoubtedly spent a lot of time and effort thinking about the details of it: how it will work, why it will be good for everyone involved, how it will be successful, and what the end reward will be. The challenge now is to condense everything that you've done and thought into something that you can show or tell other people so that they get the same degree of enthusiasm. It's difficult, but that's your challenge. Keep in mind that other people whose help you need are starting off cold. They haven't spent the weeks or the months living with this project that you have. To get them to share in your dream, you have to come up with a way of making it interesting to them. This is called *showmanship*—and it is one of Trump's signature traits.

One great example of Trump's showmanship was his hiring of Henry Pearce, a dignified, New York City banker with decades of experience, to assist him in obtaining the financing for the Commodore. Trump was only 27 and he knew bankers would be skeptical of lending so much money to someone so young. Showmanship, in this case, meant conveying a powerful symbol of reliability and safety to the conservative bankers, and this is exactly what Trump did when he sat down at the table with Pearce at his side. Instead of seeing a 27-year-old asking for millions of dollars, the bankers saw Trump with someone they had been dealing with for years—even though the reality was that he was just a temporary hired gun for Trump.

An even better example of Trump's showmanship is the way he used flashy architecture to get people excited about the Commodore-Hyatt deal. Using eye-catching, conversation-starting architecture is one of Trump's signature tactics, and it's something every real estate investor, no matter how small, should consider doing. A good design and some flashy ideas from an architect can easily add far more value to a project than the cost of the architect's fee. If you can create something impressive and distinctive, you will be able to get premium rents or a premium selling price for your property.

Trump felt that the Commodore was going down hill because it looked so dark and dingy. His plan was to build a new façade directly over the building's old skeletal structure in glass, or bronze if that was feasible, otherwise he would demolish the existing building and build a new one. It had to embody "showmanship"—a building with sparkle and excitement that would make people stop and notice. He hired a young, talented architect named Der Scutt, to help him realize this vision.

Next, Trump used showmanship to get New York City to agree to a massive 40-year tax abatement in order to make this deal work, and instead, take a share of the profits. This was a critical piece of his plan. But Trump knew that convincing the politicians and bureaucrats in New York City government to go along with this plan would be extremely difficult. To imagine that the run-down Commodore Hotel, mostly vacant and mired in unpaid property taxes, could evolve into one of the busiest and most luxurious hotels in

Manhattan was a tough proposition for anyone to believe. He had to give the Board of Estimate something physical to look at, to touch, in order to make his vision real.

Trump had the architect come up with sketches and renderings that he could use in his presentations to the city and the lenders. He told Der to make it appear that he had spent a huge sum of money on the drawings. A beautiful presentation can be very impressive. It worked. People began to believe in the idea.

How Small Investors Can Use Showmanship

There are plenty of inexpensive ways to use showmanship in small real estate investments. For example, instead of showing prospective buyers a vacant piece of land, show them a rendering of what the project will look like after it is built. Hire an artist if necessary. It may be worth investing in a scale model of your property so that buyers can visualize the final product.

Also, how you dress, your appearance, says something to the people you're trying to influence. Donald Trump always dresses in a way that will make a good impression on the people whose help he needs. To spearhead a luxury hotel deal in the heart of Manhattan, a pinstripe suit and silk tie are the safest bet. But because appearance communicates adaptability as well as respectability, Trump knows that khakis and a polo shirt are appropriate for golf course negotiations, or a hard hat for on-site construction projects. Your dress should be chosen to give people confidence that you can do what you say you're going to do.

Think about the people whose help you need to make your investment successful. When meeting with a bank you may want to wear a suit—but very high heels or excessive makeup might compromise the impression you want to make. If you're meeting with a contractor, try to keep it casual, don't overdress, but try to wear a casual outfit that still looks impressive. First impressions make a powerful statement.

BE BETTER PREPARED THAN ANYONE ELSE

Most people don't realize that there's a lot of preparation involved in getting people to respond in the way you want them to respond. The key is anticipating problems and questions that other people will ask about your proposal and having answers ready. Donald Trump spends significant amounts of time preparing for important meetings in which he needs to persuade a key person or group.

Here's an example for small investors: You want to sell a home to a potential buyer. The buyer says that he wants to buy the house, but his purchase will be subject to getting a mortgage. Here is where your planning pays off. If you have already done your homework and contacted a bank, which has agreed to make a mortgage on the house for x amount of dollars, you anticipated this potential problem. Now you can tell the buyer, "I already have the ideal bank for you to go to." I have now directed you to one source, instead of you going to ten sources and getting confused.

You could be selling a house with a very old refrigerator, and you don't want to buy a new one. You anticipate a buyer's objection by saying (if the objection comes up), "I'll guarantee that if the refrigerator doesn't last a year, I'll buy you a new one." You have anticipated a potential problem. So instead of the buyer asking for a discount because he wants a new refrigerator, you simply give him a one-year warranty. Whatever the situation, whether you are buying or selling, try to anticipate any likely potential problem.

You do this by taking an objective look at what it is you're trying to accomplish. You say, "If I were the buyer, what would I find objectionable?" Put yourself in the shoes of the other party and raise the questions they would raise, then find the answers to the questions. There's always some wrinkle in the transaction, something that you will need to address so that you can quickly move on so the other party doesn't dwell on it. Keep your goal in mind and think through any potential obstacles and have possible solutions ready.

If you are preparing for a meeting, you need to think about how you can use the meeting to build rapport, but also focus on what your objective is. Perhaps you want others to invest; maybe you want them to accept your capabilities, whatever the case you must prepare for that meeting: What you're going to say; what you're going to do; and who the audience is; who you'll be playing to. This way you can have the maximum effect. If you don't prepare, you'll fall flat.

There was a researcher named Ziff who made a study of negotiation. He expanded a concept called *Ziff's principle of least effort,* which proved that most people will put the least amount of effort in a transaction that they can in order to proceed. When I read about the theory, I immediately realized it was true in real estate. Most people are not willing to put in a lot of time to prepare before making big real estate decisions, and you can make this work to your advantage if you are willing to do what most other people won't. Knowing that others want to put in very little effort, successful people like Trump take the role of filling the gap and doing all of the effort that's required in a transaction. They do it on behalf of the other people involved in the transaction who don't want to do it. Trump always does more preparation than other people are willing to because it gives him greater control in a fluid situation.

For example, if Trump is creating a plan to attract investors in a property, knowing what he does about human nature, he's not going to expect you to spend a lot of time and effort reading the details. He'll do all the mathematics for you in the plan and at the bottom he'll write, in big type, "Return on your money: 20% a year." Most people are going to go right to that "20% a year." They're not going to delve into the details. They're enamored with the 20%.

When Trump has a person interested in a transaction, he will do everything he can to make his involvement in that transaction easy. For example, "I'll do this so you don't have to; I'll send you this; I'll take care of that phone call." You want to keep other people, as much as possible, *out* of the nitty gritty of the actual transaction, so you can control the details. Take advantage of the fact that most people are not willing to spend time on preparation.

Trump spent huge amounts of time preparing for the New York City Board of Estimate, which first met to approve his entire Commodore transaction in late December 1975. One of the things he did a week beforehand, was to go to Victor Palmieri, the executive from Penn Central Railroad who owned the Commodore Hotel and explain to him that if he wanted the city to take our abatement case seriously, we needed to get out the message that the Commodore was going downhill fast and that it was not going to survive much longer. Palmieri agreed with him. On December 12, Palmieri made a public announcement to the media that the Commodore Hotel had lost another $1.2 million during 1975, was anticipating worse losses in 1976, and as a result intended to shut down the hotel permanently no later then June 30, 1976. This announcement by itself didn't change the Board of Estimate's mind, but they agreed to hold several more meetings with Trump. However, from the beginning of negotiations, the single event that nobody in city government wanted to see was the Commodore closed down and boarded up. So the news release prior to the December meeting helped get the Board of Estimates worried about a closing of the Commodore. Then, next spring, on May 12, 1976, one week before the Board of Estimate, for the fourth time, was to vote on Trump's tax abatement, Trump got Palmieri to announce that Penn Central would permanently close the Commodore in six days. Palmieri explained to the media that the occupancy had decreased from 46 percent the previous year to 33 percent, and that operational losses for 1976 were projected at $4.6 million.

Adding fuel to the fire, on May 19, was the front-page news in all the local newspapers about the remaining tenants being forced out of the Commodore. The news featured stories about the hundreds of employees who were now looking for work, and the dismay the local retailers were feeling in anticipation of a boarded-up Commodore Hotel.

On May 20, thanks in part to Trump's strategic preparations for his four meetings with the Board of Estimate, the Board finally voted unanimously to give Trump the full tax abatement deal he had sought. Over the 40-year term, the tax abatement saved him tens of millions of dollars. This is typical of how Trump thinks strategically about preparing for critical meetings. He will go to great lengths to create conditions that will work to his favor during the meeting.

How Small Investors Can Use Preparation to Their Advantage

Suppose, for example, you need a temporary construction loan for a fixer-upper. Before you ever ask for a loan, talk to other people who have received construction loans. What did they have to do to qualify? What kind of fees and rates did the lender charge? Were they happy with the lender? Do as much networking as you can to find people who have direct experience and are knowledgeable about the kind of loan you want, and who can give you the inside story on what it takes to get that kind of a loan with favorable terms. Getting information from insiders or people who know more than you is the best kind of preparation you can do for an important meeting or negotiation.

Preparation is important in all phases of a real estate investment. It shows up in how well conceived your plan for fixing up and selling a property is, and how many contingencies you have prepared for; it's in how you present yourself to a lender and if you have properly anticipated answering the wide range of questions a lender might ask; it's in how you talk about your property in different ways, to the different people you're trying to sell (the banker, the investors, the building department, etc.). You need to plan for how to emphasize different elements of the project to each constituency, depending on what is important to them. Preparation means finding out what they are likely to want from the deal and figuring out how you can give it to them, while still getting what you want.

Preparation could involve taking a real estate agent out to lunch. Or showing him another property that you've bought and sold that reflects what you want to accomplish. You can prepare for answering questions about the costs of your project by looking hard until you find another building that was recently renovated and reflects what you want to accomplish. Show it to your contractor, and tell him, "Look, I have this in mind." You will learn a great deal about the risks, expenses, and feasibility of your idea. But in order to do that, you have to prepare by finding a comparable building to look at.

You can't spend too much time preparing. If you go into a meeting without preparing, you will have no advantage over the people you are dealing with, and you will not be in control of the situation. The more planning and preparation that you have, the greater the degree of success.

BE TENACIOUS

Anytime you are dealing with the huge investments of time and money that real estate represents, you are also dealing with people who believe in maintaining the status quo for the property, or who just don't have any particular interest in helping you improve the property. You are going to have to be tenacious to get anything done. If it's easy, there's probably not a lot of profit in it. Trump's most profitable projects have been those such as 40 Wall Street (to be discussed later in the book) where he picked up a property for very little because a string of earlier investors had failed with the property—and only he had the tenacity and vision to make it work. Everything that is really successful was the result of hard work that nobody else wanted to do. The only thing that held the whole Commodore-Hyatt deal together was Trump's tenacity—he was like a hungry pit bull.

For example, during early negotiations with New York City over the Commodore Hotel, one of the city's key concerns was who would run this new hotel. They said, "You say you're going to pay us rent, and that you're going to give us a share of the profits, but what do you, Donald Trump, know about running a first-class hotel?" And at first, he didn't have an answer. But he said, "All right, I'll go out and get a major player to run it." And the city responded with, "Okay, if you bring in a major hotel operator, we'll go along with it." That tentative commitment from the city gave him a strong position from which to negotiate with a hotel company, and he ended up bringing in Hyatt as a partner. Once again his tenacity helped him turn a roadblock into an additional benefit for this investment.

One of the biggest roadblocks the small investor will encounter is the mortgage lender. Tenacity can help a lot here. If the first lender you approach denies you a loan, keep trying with other lenders. Make inquiries with friends and neighbors about who is making mortgage loans in your neighborhood. If you look hard enough, you will find a lender, though you may have to pay a premium for the loan.

Another potential roadblock could be a stubborn seller. Here you have to find out exactly why he or she does not want to sell, then in a determined way, answer each issue.

Other possible roadblocks could be denial of a zoning variance or a building permit. Again, you have to approach the problem tenaciously. Find out what the bureaucrats' specific concerns with your plans are, then address these issues.

Everything worth doing is difficult, and in order to accomplish it, you have to be tenacious.

SUMMARY

I deliberately started this book with a chapter on personal qualities because most people don't realize the role that people skills play in real estate investing success. It is not just a matter of financing, buying the right property, getting tenants, and so on. All these elements are built on a foundation of having the right personal qualities. Great real estate investors like Trump are also great entrepreneurs. They know that they know how to get people excited about their bold ideas, and they are undaunted by the setbacks, problems, and disappointments that cause most people to give up.

2

THINK BIG

How Trump Chooses
Properties to Invest In

KEY POINTS

- Be willing to pay a premium for a prime location.
- Don't buy without a creative vision for adding significant value.
- Four things Trump looks for in a location.
- Creative problem solving leads to big profits.
- Write a preliminary business plan before you buy.

Y OU'VE HEARD THE cliche about the three most important things in real estate being "location, location, location." Trump thinks this is misleading. Location is important, but having a great location doesn't guarantee anything. It's a starting point for what could be a great investment. However, an inept real estate investor could own property at a great location and lose a fortune. One of the cornerstones of Trump's philosophy is "Improve any Location." In other words, use creativity and vision to change the way your location is utilized. Trump never gets involved with something that's just ordinary—it has to be very special. If he's building an apartment building, it has to be the most luxurious, and the biggest and best in the area. Small investors can adapt this principle by doing something radical to their property, changing the zoning, changing the way the property is used, or renovating it so strikingly that people think about the location in a new way. That's what he decided to do when he conceived the idea for Trump World Tower at the United Nations Plaza.

DEAL CASE STUDY

TRUMP WORLD TOWER AT THE UNITED NATIONS

When Donald first discovered this property in 1997 it contained a sprawling two-story building situated across the street from the United Nations in New York City. The building was the headquarters of an engineering society whose officers decided to sell the building because the value of land for new construction had skyrocketed, and given the prime location they believed they could get a high price and move their offices into better space nearer the business hub of New York City. The zoning ordinance affecting the site limited the size of any new building on the property to a 10:1 ratio: Any new structure could be no bigger than 10 times the square-footage of the land. Since the land area was approximately 37,000 square feet this would have limited Trump to constructing a 370,000 square foot building on the site. Trump knew that the property was very expensive but it was an entire block from 47th Street to 48th Street with an unparalleled view of the United Nations headquarters and the East River. He felt he had to build something extraordinary that would justify the high price of the land and take advantage of the sight lines of the property. Fortuitously, the existing zoning covering the property permitted the transfer of unused "air rights" from one parcel of land to a contiguous parcel on the same block. When the city wrote its zoning law, it wanted to limit the amount of bulk on a particular block but not necessarily building height. It didn't care if the bulk was in one building or 20 buildings. In other words, if a building on Parcel A was 10,000 square feet but the zoning permitted a 30,000-square-foot building, the owner of Parcel A could sell the excess 20,000 square feet of building coverage ("air rights") to the owner of Parcel B. In fact, the building department liked the idea of the bulk being in one structure because it gave you more light and air everywhere else in the neighborhood. Since there was little likelihood that the owner of the unused air rights would ever use them, their sale to an adjoining owner who wanted them could fetch a price far in excess of their worth to the owner who had them.

After making preliminary evaluations, Trump, "thinking big" as he typically does, decided to build a huge luxury condominium tower using air rights from adjoining underbuilt properties. No other developer recognized this possibility, and it was the key to Trump turning this "ordinary" property into something extraordinary. But the process

Trump World Tower at United Nations Plaza

would be extremely difficult. First, Trump would have to agree to buy the engineering society's property. Then he would have to convince the owners of the adjacent properties to sell him their unused air rights. In complete compliance with the law, Trump could then incorporate these air rights with the parcel he was buying and get a building permit for a much larger building. If he could buy enough air rights, he could build something really unique—the tallest residential building in New York City.

The key to making this concept work was to acquire the air rights of adjacent buildings *quietly*. Building owners in New York City with excess air rights are often willing to sell them freely because they consider the dollars they get for the air rights as "found money." But if word got out to nearby building owners about what Trump was doing, the prices for those air rights on parcels on the same block might have escalated through the roof. A difficult problem to be overcome was that only air rights on contiguous parcels were of value. He had to make a deal for the air rights on one parcel adjoining the one he was buying, and then work his way down the block to acquire the air rights on several parcels that adjoined one another. So he took options on various properties, offering the owners a high price, subject to his ability to acquire the air rights needed to form the chain permitted by the zoning. The outright purchase of all the adjacent parcels was impossible because one of the parcels was a church that might be willing to sell its air rights but never the church.

Thus, we had several negotiations going on concurrently, and we had to conduct all the negotiations secretly. To help keep our negotiations for air rights simple, we offered the same price per square foot for the air rights to all adjoining property owners. If one owner got a higher price per square foot, we agreed that all other owners would get that same price. That way no owner could feel cheated. In some cases, we actually told an owner, "This is the price per square foot we agreed to pay John Smith for his air rights, and we are offering you the same deal."

Having assembled air rights from seven adjoining parcels, we applied to the building department for a building permit to build a towering 677,000-square-foot building with 376 condominium units—the tallest residential building in New York City. We showed the City that we were in full compliance with the zoning resolutions and were entitled to the issuance of a building permit. We would be building as "a matter of right" meaning we didn't need any special permission from the zoning board. The building department of the City of New York agreed. Some representatives said, "We might not like the proposed building, but it's perfectly legal to build it." They felt that if they denied issuing a building permit, their denial would be overturned in court and possibly lead to a huge damage award.

So, the building department issued the permit. Trump immediately began construction. He did this to gain the advantage of having already broken ground, in the event a lawsuit was filed seeking an injunction against construction.

As the scope of the building as the tallest residential building in New York City and maybe the entire world became evident, a number of prominent residents in the community decided to oppose it. They tried to use political pressure but were told Trump was acting well within the law. A group of wealthy residents in the area, including Walter Cronkite, filed a lawsuit to stop construction, arguing that "the zoning in this neighborhood was intended to permit something completely different; you can't build a 90-floor monster right in front of the U.N." We explained that it wasn't 90 floors, it was 72 floors (it was 90 stories *high* because of higher than normal ceiling heights (ceiling heights did not affect permitted square footage). The opposition didn't like that fact either, but what we did was entirely within the law.

It is easy to understand that when this lawsuit was filed to stop the building, the lenders who had agreed to finance the construction of the building got nervous. They felt that there was a real possibility that the building might never be built as Trump envisioned it. But Trump had a Plan B. He established a relationship with Daewoo— one of the largest corporations in Korea—who was willing to be his partner and would guarantee repayment of the loan if the planned building did not materialize. So now the mortgage lender wasn't worried about the adverse publicity or the lawsuit because they had this billion dollar company, Daewoo, which is the equivalent of General Motors in Korea, to guarantee repayment of the loan if necessary.

Meanwhile, the building kept going up. The opposition tried to stop the construction. They claimed that if Trump's building was allowed to be built they would lose their beautiful views of the East River. They filed a lawsuit against Donald Trump and the City of New York for wrongfully issuing the building permit; but Trump filed a countersuit that sought damages as a result of the opposition's lawsuit and a judgment that the building permit was properly issued. The court basically ruled that the city had every right to issue the permit and Mr. Trump had every right to build the building under the permit. They were not going to issue an injunction in this case because the damages would be horrendous and it was unlikely that Trump's position would be overturned on appeal. They allowed the construction to proceed.

The opposition lost in the lower courts and eventually took their lawsuit to the Court of Appeals—the highest New York State court. The Court of Appeals didn't even review the case to consider overturning it. Their comment to the plaintiffs was, "If you don't like the zoning law, change it. But any subsequent change to the zoning law will not affect this building which is being built in accordance with the law as it now exists."

Trump World Tower is now one of the most luxurious residential towers in the world and enjoys a five-star rating. Many of the apartments have maids' rooms, wood-burning fireplaces, and 16-foot ceilings. A four-bedroom condominium sells for as much as $13.5 million. The building was a huge success and the construction loan was paid off long before its due date from the sale proceeds from units.

Ironically, once the Trump World Tower was completed, some of the people who fought the construction because it blocked their views bought units in Trump World Tower because of its superior construction and far superior views.

PRINCIPLE 1: BE WILLING TO PAY A PREMIUM FOR A PRIME LOCATION

BY GEORGE . . . A STORY OF SMART OVERPAYMENT

Perhaps the best example of paying a premium price for a piece of real estate occurred in 1962 when I was counsel for Sol Goldman and Alex DiLorenzo Jr., the multimillionaires I worked for early in my career. Since they were considered to be the most aggressive purchasers of real estate, they would get dozens of listings sent to them every day. Part of my job was to screen the sale offers and get Sol's opinion as to which ones were of interest to him. One day, a disheveled old broker came into my office and handed me a crumpled piece of paper listing an apartment house in Brooklyn Heights that was for sale by the family who had built it and owned it for over 40 years. The asking price was $860,000 which, at that time, was a lot of money. I didn't know whether the price was high or low but I did know that Brooklyn Heights was a desirable neighborhood, so I brought the listing into Goldman. I told him the broker was a "nobody" and I doubted his

(Continued)

ability to bring in anything worthwhile but I thought it was worth bringing it to Sol's attention. Goldman took a quick look at the listing and said, "George, find out how many people the broker has offered this apartment house to." I did as I was asked and when I went back into Sol's office I said, "He knows you're the number one buyer of property in Brooklyn so you are the first person who is aware of this offer." After listening to me, Sol said to me, "I know everything about this property, the type of apartments, the rentals, how well it was built and operated, and I have been secretly trying to buy it for years without success. If the listing gets out in the maketplace, a bidding war will take place for the property and I want to avoid that at all costs. Go out and tell the broker your odd-ball client will pay $1 million for the property." I said, "Sol, they're only asking $860,000 for the building, so you could probably buy it for $825,000, why offer $1 million?" Sol insisted that I do as he directed. I pleaded, "How can I possibly get the broker to understand the excessive offer." Sol said, "Hey, you're the lawyer, be creative." I went back to the broker who was still sitting in my office and said, "My client likes the property but there is a serious problem. The price is too low!" Thinking he heard wrong the broker said, "You might be able to buy it for $820,000 if you move quickly." I replied, "You're going in the wrong direction, unless you up the price to $1 million my client isn't interested." The broker had a look of total bewilderment on his face and asked, "Why would anyone pay $1 million for a piece of property that could be bought for $860,000?" I replied, "My client is a very eccentric millionaire, he thinks anything that costs less than $1 million is beneath him. So if you come back with a sales contract indicating a purchase price of $1 million, I'm authorized to sign it and give you a deposit of $100,000 immediately. But, I suggest you move quickly before my client comes to his senses." The broker came back with the contract the next day; I signed it and gave him the deposit. The amazing thing is that before title had even passed, Goldman obtained a first mortgage on the property from a bank for $1.4 million—the property was that good. So Sol now owned a building he always coveted, and had pocketed $400,000. The seemingly exorbitant price in reality was an incredible bargain. By overpaying, he made sure the property stayed off the market. There's an excellent lesson here for the small investor. If your instinct tells you a piece of real estate has your name on it, and is significantly undervalued, go for it and forget the price tag!

There will always be a demand for a prime location, and people will always pay a premium price to get a prime location. You have to avoid the trap of looking only at the average selling prices in your local real estate marketplace, and be willing to "overpay" if overpayment is warranted. In other words, the so-called "average market price" of property is computed based on limited general information relating to an entire neighborhood, not the value of a specific property which may have a desirable size and a better location. You may have to pay 50 percent to 100 percent more to get a good property in a great location, but it's worth it if that will allow you to attract superior tenants or buyers, and if you can improve the site to get maximum value out of it.

Trump World Tower was a perfect example of overpaying for a prime location. When Trump found it, the property contained an outdated two-story office building owned by an engineering fraternity. The amount of money they wanted for the site was outrageous. But Donald Trump paid it, because he knew other buildings on the block had unused air rights that could be purchased at reasonable prices and then he could build something extraordinary.

Trump is always willing to pay a premium for a prime location, but he also knows that "there's no right price for the wrong property." He will not buy something just because it's cheap, if he can't see a way to add significant value. The reality is that in small or large ways, each property is unique and is actually worth more or less than the average selling price for other buildings in its neighborhood. For example, 450 Park Avenue in Manhattan is a great location, and theoretically should command high rents that would translate into a high selling price. But (and this is a huge "but"), the building was built with an unusual facade with curved windows. It might be beautiful to look at from the street, but the windows are oddly shaped and at a peculiar height in reference to the floor and ceiling. Also, the perimeter heating was not installed against the exterior wall and juts into the usable floorspace. Because of the curvature of the walls and windows, the interior did not lay out well for offices. What you have is an office building with low ceilings, inefficient space utilization, and awkward windows. In this situation, even though the building might command a high price considering the Park Avenue address, it's still the wrong building. You could never get really high rents for space in this building unless you did a complete makeover, which would be tremendously expensive. It's an office building that can't work as a premium office building. The moral is, don't buy property just because you think you can get it at a bargain price.

PRINCIPLE 2: DON'T BUY WITHOUT A CREATIVE VISION FOR ADDING SIGNIFICANT VALUE TO A PROSPECTIVE PROPERTY

As I said before, if you are planning on buying a top-notch location, you'll normally pay a premium for it. If you intend to proceed with the acquisition, ask yourself, "How can I justify the overpayment?" For starters, if you have a prime location you can probably get prime tenants. But that's usually not enough to warrant the premium you must pay. Trump will only pay a premium for real estate in a great location if he can devise a plan that will dramatically change the way people perceive and value the property. To be attractive to Trump or to any intelligent investor there has to be undiscovered potential for adding significant value to the property—value that is not already factored into the selling price of the building.

For example, if the officers of the engineering society had known that it was possible to build a 90-story building on their property they could have sold the concept to many other developers for a much higher price. Most people looking at the site would have seen only the potential for a 370,000-square-foot 20-story building, the limit permitted under the then existing zoning restrictions of the city. What made the deal successful was Trump's creative vision for buying up the surrounding air rights, and using them to build a towering 667,000 square foot structure with high ceilings, floor-to-ceiling windows, thus capitalizing on the site's potentially magnificent views. The genius of Trump was that he was able to put all the pieces together at a price that was consistent with the anticipated sales prices he would get for the condominium units.

Though you may be a small investor, if you want to be extremely successful make sure that you too have a vision for adding significant value to any property you buy. Think about your vision for adding undiscovered value before you get serious about putting any money down for the property. You have to think creatively about the ways to get the highest and best use out of a property. For example, you might buy a fixer-upper in a great neighborhood and renovate it, or build an addition, increase the number of units or the quality of the tenants. Other creative options are to build another building or amenities on the property, change the use from residential to commercial or vice versa, or seek a variance or a change in the zoning. These are all ways to enhance the value.

The bottom line is, whenever you are considering buying an investment property; explore ways to "Improve the Location."

PRINCIPLE 3: FOUR THINGS TRUMP
LOOKS FOR IN A LOCATION

Great Views

What Trump liked best about the location on which he built Trump World Tower was the potential for stunning views over the East River. Without that, he would not have bought the property. In fact, views were also an important factor behind the success of his 40 Wall Street building (great views of New York Harbor from the upper floors), Trump Tower (which overlooks Central Park), Trump International Hotel and Tower (also overlooking Central Park), and his West Side Towers that overlook the Hudson River. For a small investor, good views may mean something slightly different, and more modest, but just as important to the value of the property. For example, a modest residential building may have views onto a grove of trees at the back of the property. Turning them into a park-like setting could raise the value of the building. In one of his buildings, Trump went so far as to cut larger window holes out of the existing structure, to enhance the building's views of Central Park. The importance of views depends on the particular use of the property you have in mind. Certainly, nobody wants to live near a dumpsite or a sewerage treatment plant but a quiet street is a good view for a modest residential building. At a minimum, look for a view that is compatible with the life style of the occupants of your property and you've passed the view requirement.

Prestige

Trump also looks for locations that have prestige, and in the case of Trump World Tower, he liked the prestige of having a building next to the United Nations. Trump knew that many governments would be eager to buy luxury apartments for their senior diplomats across the street from the UN building. Trump Tower has a 5th Avenue address which is very prestigious as is the Wall Street address of the Trump building at 40 Wall Street. A small investor purchasing a real estate parcel should consider whether or not the location or the address is desirable for the people you intend to attract. If your target is high-income families, then you have to buy in an area that already contains luxury residences. If your intended target is middle-income families or low-income families, pick an area considered to be desirable among members of that group.

Growth Potential

Any real estate acquisition by Trump must have some growth potential or it won't pique his interest. The most important questions to be answered are: "Will this investment keep up with changing times? Will rents keep up with inflation? Is the area stable, getting better, or deteriorating?" Any serious investor in real estate should be asking and answering the very same questions if you expect to be successful. One of the best places to look for undervalued property is in marginal areas that are near very successful locations.

Land banking may be appropriate in many cases. Land banking is buying land on the theory that, in time, it's going to go up in value, perhaps because it's in a strategic location. Meanwhile, you're going to pay the taxes and other carrying charges on it. To the extent you have no offsetting income—that's your investment. You may not intend to develop it or build on it yourself. Your intention may be to own it until the value of its location increases. In New York City, a good example of land banking might be acquiring an existing parking lot in the midst of surrounding underutilized parcels. Your immediate intention might be to continue the property's interim use as a parking lot, until a more profitable use comes into view.

Land banking is always a risky investment but one that can be extremely profitable if you guess right. It's a good idea to go into land banking with money you're willing to lose or tie up for a long time. It works especially well when there's an area or neighborhood that is in transition, or it looks like it's in transition. For example, you see a depressed area, and an area not far away which is starting to flourish, being rebuilt, and on the rise. You might say to yourself, "Hey, I can buy here while it's cheap, because sooner or later the growth will come my way and I want to be there when it happens." So you buy on the theory that there will be an uptick at some time in the foreseeable future. You never know how long it will take for that to occur. You have no control over if it happens or when it happens. However one thing is for sure. The earlier you buy it, the cheaper the price and conversely, the later you buy it—once the growth in the neighborhood gets hot—the higher the price.

Convenience

Another thing Trump looks for in a location is the convenience of the location for his intended customers whether they are apartment owners or office tenants. Convenience encompasses the proximity of shopping facilities, transportation, schools, houses of worship, and other amenities. Availability of a suitable labor force is a factor to be considered in determining the desirability of office or commercial space. If you intend to live or work in the property you are planning to buy, just ask yourself does this property meet your needs; can you picture yourself being happy there and in the neighborhood. If the answer is "yes" it should be a good buy. Your future buyers will probably have the same response. If it's not a place you would feel comfortable, I suggest you pass.

PRINCIPLE 4: CREATIVE PROBLEM SOLVING
LEADS TO BIG PROFITS

In my 20 years of representing major estate developers before I met Donald Trump I earned my reputation as a problem solver, and it's one of the reasons he hired me. It has been the key to my success in real estate and in law, and I encourage every small real estate investor to think of real estate problems, especially in the acquisition stage, as "opportunities." In fact, Donald and I both tend to view things that are considered "impossible" by other experts, as simply taking longer. This is what happened on the Commodore Hotel deal I described in Chapter 1, and this common perspective has been one of the foundations of our work together. We became a formidable combination that still exists today.

As I mentioned, one of the things I learned from working with New York real estate mogul Sol Goldman, is that "every problem has a price tag." Many small real estate investors are intimidated by problems, but to entrepreneurial minds like Trump's, a problem is like a key to the vault—a reason to get an even lower price on a building. Some of Trump's biggest profits have come from properties he bought cheap because they had complex problems nobody had been able to solve. After he solved the problem, he reaped millions of dollars in profits (40 Wall Street, which I discuss in Chapter 3, is a good example). Ambitious real estate investors should look at a problem property (provided it can be bought at a correspondingly large discount) as a great opportunity.

Unfortunately, lawyers are too often trained to kill deals when problems arise, rather than translating legal problems and risks into financial terms, so that a business decision can be made. Many times real estate deals run into problems that can only be solved with creative, "out-of-the-box" thinking. That's how Donald and I put together a deal that brought Niketown to a prime location in New York City.

Creative Problem Solving: Trump, Ross, IBM, and the Nike Building on 5th Avenue

In the process of putting together the property to build Trump Tower (I tell that story in Chapter 5), Trump acquired the Bonwit Teller building on 5th Avenue. However, the ground lease for this site was owned by a veteran New York investor named Leonard Kandell. Bonwit Teller was leasing the site for a below-market rent and in 1990 fell on hard times. They wanted out of their lease and were willing to pay for the privilege. Gallerie Lafayette, a premier French department store chain wanted a New York store, so Trump sold them on the idea of taking over the Bonwit Teller store—at a rent which topped the old Bonwit rent by over $3 million a year! He then agreed to cancellation of the Bonwit lease and Bonwit paid a few million to get off the obligation. The success Gallerie Lafayette envisioned never happened and in 1993–1994 they too wanted out and were also willing to pay for the privilege. At that time, Nike desired to build a flagship store on 57th Street. The Bonwit/Lafayette/Kandell site with its 50-foot frontage was too small but Trump also had a long-term lease on a site owned by IBM that was next to the Kandell site and also had 50 feet of frontage. Trump asked Nike, "If I can combine both sites giving you 100 feet of frontage and 100 feet of depth would you agree to a long-term lease?" Nike loved the idea and agreed to a rent averaging $9 million a year. They also agreed to demolish the buildings on both sites and then construct a new $50 million Niketown building at their own expense. Now the problem Trump was faced with was convincing two separate ground lease owners (Kandell and IBM) to revise and extend their ground leases with Trump to permit Nike to build. Trump had previously been a long-term client of mine but I hadn't represented him for seven years. At that time, I was the attorney for Leonard Kandell. Trump sent two of his associates to renegotiate the Kandell ground lease with me. Although I wasn't working for Donald, I wanted to be helpful if it benefited Kandell. Trump's representatives said that they felt the Kandell site had a value of $2.5 million and they were willing to pay a rent starting at $250,000 a year. I told them I couldn't agree with the value they placed on the site because there was one "0" missing. $25 million was the right number. They were shocked by my answer and went back to report to Trump their lack of success. They complained, "You told us we could make a fair deal with George Ross but what he wants is outrageous." When they told Trump the offer they had made, he said, "What did you expect? You tried to low ball him and he did you one better. I'll handle it myself."

Donald called me and arranged a meeting. At that meeting he told me about the Nike deal and asked me what I could do to help him do it. Once again I was impressed with the creative problem-solving genius of Trump in envisioning this complex plan. I told him if the increased rental was adequate I could get Kandell to agree to a revised lease that would enable the Nike deal to be made, but obtaining a revision of the IBM lease was his problem and Ed Minskoff who represented IBM would be very difficult to convince. I was right. Minskoff raised obstacles that were difficult or impossible to overcome, such as asking for control of the Kandell site. As each problem arose Trump would call me and ask my advice. I said to him, "Donald, what you need is to get Minskoff to agree to a co-ownership agreement which sets forth the rights of Kandell and IBM when the Nike lease expires." Donald said, "I've never seen a co-ownership agreement." I replied, "Neither did I until I needed one years ago and couldn't find anyone who did one. I spent a full month drafting one which touches all the bases." I told him I would send it to him and if Minskoff wanted to modify it, he could call me. Minskoff liked the co-ownership idea and told Trump if they could agree to a revision and extension of Trump's lease with IBM he had a deal. Trump and Minskoff agreed to terms and the Nike building became a very profitable reality. As is so often typical in real estate investing, this deal would have failed at many points without continuous creative problem solving.

BY GEORGE . . . CREATIVE PROBLEM
SOLVING AT OLYMPIC TOWER ON 5TH AVENUE

As I mentioned earlier, I learned how to stop thinking like a lawyer and think like a problem solver while I worked for Sol Goldman, who forced me to put a price on every real estate problem. In the early 1970s, my problem-solving expertise eventually endeared me to Arthur Cohen, another creative genius where real estate was involved, and principal of Arlen Realty and Development Corporation, a publicly traded entity. Cohen came up with the original idea of erecting a mixed-use building on 51st Street and 5th Avenue in New York City with stores on the ground floor, offices above for approximately 20 floors, and finally topped by another 20 floors containing luxury cooperative apartments. However, the only property he could control was a narrow plot in the middle of the block. The plot fronted on 5th Avenue and was occupied by Olympic Airways, a company that was owned by Aristotle Onassis. Cohen's original idea was to buy the air rights over Best & Co. which owned a large parcel of land on the corner of 5th Avenue and 51st Street. Then he would also buy the air rights over the Cartier building on 5th Avenue and 52nd Street. The Olympic site would be used for elevators to a sky lobby servicing a new building that would cantilever over the Best & Co. building. I christened this novelty building the "popsicle." But it never came to pass. Instead something else interesting happened on the site.

Cohen became a close friend of Meshulam Riklis who owned Best & Co. Riklis agreed to sell Cohen the Best & Co. site so that a normal looking building called Olympic Tower could now be built on the site—but only if I could resolve a dispute that arose between Riklis and Aristotle Onassis, each of whom wanted office space on the highest floors of the new building. Since Riklis was committing to lease several floors as part of the sale of the Best & Co. site, he insisted on taking the top four floors. But Onassis's ego would not tolerate his offices being lower than Riklis. I had to find a way to appease both of these men or the project would abort. So I sold them on the idea of checkerboarding their space. Onassis would lease the top floor. Riklis would lease the floor below. Then Onassis would lease the next lower floor until the each had the amount of space they wanted. It was a cumbersome solution but they bought it and Arthur Cohen's vision became reality. This is the kind of creative problem solving successful real estate investors need to learn to do.

As it turned out, the project needed more creative approaches to challenges and opportunities that arose. Olympic Tower was the first mixed-use building of its type in New York City. Cohen took advantage of a statute that permitted a larger building if a public area was provided on the street level. (I helped Trump do the same thing years later in Trump Tower, described in Chapter 5.) Cohen also filed for the benefits of 421a, a statute that gave favorable tax treatment for a new building built on undeveloped land. (Again Trump would do the same thing for Trump Tower.)

While Olympic Tower was being constructed, the concept of condominium ownership was gaining popularity. The idea of owning a unit rather than renting one under a lease from a cooperative corporation had merit since the unit would be taxed separately, could be easily mortgaged or sold, and would be entitled to the tax treatment available to real estate owners. One day, Arthur Cohen called me and said, "George, I'd like to turn Olympic Tower into a mixed-use condominium, can it be done?" I said, "Arthur, I never heard of such a thing, but let me check it out and see what I can come up with." I paid a visit to the New York City Building Department to see if there was any prohibition to such a building. I was told there is no statute either permitting it or prohibiting it, and they would review any building plans that were submitted. Since the state attorney general's office must approve any condominium plan or cooperative plan, I had the partner in my firm that handles such plans find out from his contact with the attorney general's office whether a mixed-use condominium plan would be acceptable. He reported back that none had ever been filed but there was no prohibition for a mixed-use building but any condominium on leased land was prohibited.

(Continued)

Relying on this information, I told Arthur the condominium plan was possible. I told my partner to draft the condominium documents. In the middle of drafting them, he asked, "I have to prepare an estimate of expenses that each unit owner will pay. What number should I use for real estate taxes?" I didn't have any idea of the thinking of the tax assessor's office as to allocation of the taxes on the land, so I paid the tax assessor a visit to get the information. The tax assessor said, "I don't have the slightest idea since the question has never come up. As of today, there are no mixed-use condominium buildings in the city. Figure it out for yourself but my best guess would be that the land taxes would be apportioned based on the ratio that the square footage of the residential portion bears to the square footage of the nonresidential portion." If the assessor's office took that approach, the amount of land taxes the unit holders would bear for the very valuable land on which the building stood would price the units out of the market.

Now I had another obstacle to overcome. How could I reduce the exposure of the unit owners for real estate taxes? The answer was simple—eliminate their ownership of the land. But the attorney general would not approve any condominium plan for a building that does not have an ownership interest in the land on which it sits. After much thought, an innovative and unusual solution came to mind, I decided to deed to the unit holders as a group the land under the 24 columns that supported the building. I prepared and filed a deed for 24 pieces of land each being four square feet and identified with a typical metes and bounds description. Except for the 24 pieces, the unit owners had no rights to any of the land. The rest of the land was owned by the owner of the unit that covered all of the building below the residential units. My concept was accepted and the Olympic Tower was a huge success. After the Olympic Tower was completed, legislation was passed governing mixed-use condominiums and the allocation of real estate taxes. Years later, when Donald Trump decided to build Trump Tower, we drew on my Olympic Tower's experience to creatively solve problems wherever it was feasible to do so.

PRINCIPLE 5: WRITE A BUSINESS PLAN BEFORE YOU BUY

Once Trump intends to purchase a property, he has his associates prepare a projected business plan containing the following items:

- Anticipated costs of various items,
- Nature and cost of available financing,
- Estimates of income,
- A projected timeline indicating when expenses will be incurred and when income will be received.

Creating a preliminary business plan is an important discipline for you to adopt because it forces you to think through the most important elements of owning a particular piece of property. It also forces you to think of your future plans for the property, and the timing of an eventual sale. Are you looking for a safe or speculative return on your money, or are you looking for a situation in which you're going to buy and do something to it, dramatically increasing the value based on your creative vision and then sell all or part of it to make a profit? (Obviously, Trump prefers the latter approach.) The key to buying or not buying is the answer to the following question, "Does the purchase achieve the intended goal as part of your investment portfolio." Ask yourself, "Am I looking to make a capital gain? Will it be short term or long term? Am I looking to buy and hold this property as part of my estate? Am I looking for a transaction that has great tax benefits, at the expense of other monetary benefits?" It depends on the nature of your goals at that time as to whether or not a particular purchase is consistent with that goal. It's very possible, logical, and desirable for a small investor to purchase different properties with different goals.

For example, you might buy a piece of land on the outskirts of town, build it up, and plan that in three years you'll sell it and double your money. Or, in another part of the city you might buy something that can be leased to a reputable tenant giving you a safe return of 8 percent on your money. In another neighborhood, you might consider building something new from the ground up with a view toward sale, lease, or long range ownership.

Here are some questions to answer in your business plan for the property:

- How are you going to increase the value of whatever it is you intend to buy?
- What are the projected costs for refurbishment, income, and expense? Make a financial analysis of the property to find out.
- Is it going to be a short- or long-term investment? Are you planning to flip the property or buy and hold?
- How do you intend to manage the property?
- How will you finance the property? Do you intend to get investors, or finance it through a bank by yourself?
- If you need investors, how will you pitch them? What percentage return on their money will they get?
- What is your strategy and timeline for selling the property?

Careful crafting of a business plan will not only help you explain more convincingly to lenders the great plans you have for the property, it will also help you be realistic about costs, and projected profits.

3

PRINCIPLES OF NEGOTIATION

How Trump Uses Them

KEY PRINCIPLES

- Insist on negotiating directly with the decision maker, not a representative.
- Create the aura of exclusivity.
- Don't be misled by the aura of legitimacy.
- Every negotiation requires preplanning.
- Avoid a quick deal.
- The invested time principle.

THE ABILITY TO negotiate intelligently is the key to the completion of any successful real estate transaction, large or small. The problem is, the art of negotiation is far more complex than just haggling over a selling price. It's mastering preparation, knowledge of human nature, learning how to uncover and exploit weaknesses, learning special skills, and many other intricacies. Good real estate negotiation principles are developed with the aim of getting others to agree with your ideas.

If you can adopt some of the negotiation principles Donald Trump used when he bought 40 Wall Street in New York City, you will give yourself a powerful advantage in your next real estate transaction. This chapter explains five key negotiation principles from that deal. Following the case study presentation is an explanation of each principle, along with examples of how Trump used them, and how small investors can do likewise.

INVESTING CASE STUDY

TRUMP'S 40 WALL STREET BUILDING

In 1994, 40 Wall Street was a huge old building in downtown Manhattan that nobody wanted. It had over one million square feet of space in a great location, but over the years had been totally mismanaged. To make matters worse, the building was almost entirely vacant and in a state of total disrepair.

Built in the 1920s, it was once the tallest building in the world and had been a renowned New York landmark. When Trump got interested in the property, and asked me to handle the acquisition for him, the land on which the building was built was owned by a wealthy German family who had granted a long-term lease to a bank that had built the building as its headquarters.

Unfortunately, the building had a very troubled past with many building operators. At one time, Ferdinand Marcos, the infamous president of the Philippines owned it, and during his tenure the building was run into the ground. Eventually, it went into foreclosure and was sold to a member of the Resnick family who had loads of real estate experience, but who still couldn't make it work. He let it go into foreclosure and the holder of the mortgage took it back. Then it went to Kinson Group out of Hong Kong. They put millions of dollars into it, but they also failed dismally. Nobody seemed able to come up with a plan that could transform 40 Wall Street from a loser to a winner.

The underlying problem was that the ground lease (the lease for the land on which the building was built) was antiquated and contained provisions that were hostile to potential occupants, making it difficult for anyone to finance a purchase of the lease or needed building renovations. Although they tried, none of the previous owners could ever get the ground lease modified to eliminate the deficiencies it contained. Percy Pyne was the man who represented the German property owner, and nobody was able to bypass him in order to negotiate directly with the owner. Pyne was a difficult man to deal with and continually placed unacceptable obstacles in the way of every deal that was proposed.

While the Kinson group poured millions of dollars into the property, they also forced most tenants out of the building, leaving it almost vacant, except for a law firm that occupied seven floors on a long-term lease. Kinson left the building with virtually no services and in terrible shape, and to make matters worse, their failure to pay contractors resulted in the filing of several mechanic liens adding up to almost a million dollars against the building. Since there was no

40 Wall Street

better alternative, the Kinson group agreed that it would give Trump an option to buy the building for $1 million. (The huge building was one million square feet, which meant Trump could buy the building for a dollar per square foot—a ridiculously low price.) Trump also assumed liability for the $1 million of liens.

Trump realized he could never make a deal with Percy Pyne, so in a stroke of pure genius he flew to Germany and met directly with the owner of the property. He was following one of the basic principles that good salespeople know—find a way to get around the gatekeeper and talk directly to the decision maker.

Trump told the owner, "If you work with me and give me a fair ground lease, I will make 40 Wall Street a very successful building that you will be proud of. But, he added, I can't pay you any rent for at least a year while I am renovating the building. I know you have had a parade of failing tenants but I guarantee I won't join the list."

Trump won over the owner, who agreed to rewrite the lease to make it financeable and feasible for either an office or residential building.

Part of what Trump loved about this deal was the fact that no one else had been able to make the building work. He loved the challenge. What made it even more enticing was the location: it had wonderful views of the New York Harbor and fantastic potential. Also, Trump thought the rental market would turn around, the building was huge, and where in the world could you buy a prime-located office building for $1 a square foot even with all its problems? It's unheard of. Even though in 1996, the downtown New York City area was still a disaster, Trump exercised the option to buy 40 Wall Street.

Trump had an advisor named Abe Wallach who played an instrumental role in the purchase of 40 Wall Street and was of the opinion that it could never be successful as an office building. He thought the only feasible solution was a conversion into residential co-operative apartments. At this particular time, there was a glut of office space, and in fact, the city was offering developers incentives to convert vacant office space in the downtown area to residential units. So

Trump said to me, "George, I'm thinking of turning 40 Wall Street into co-op units, because that's what everybody else is doing. I want you to analyze the situation and tell me what you think I should do."

A number of well-known brokers had analyzed the building and determined that there were no tenants looking for office space downtown. They said that even if the office rental market improved, the higher floors were too small to be attractive, and the lower floors contained huge columns that interfered with efficient space usage. Their sentiments were unanimous: "It will never work as an office building even if by some miracle the market for downtown office space improves."

But there was a major roadblock to residential conversion. Before any work could be commenced a deal would have to be made with the seven-floor law firm to give up their lease. Based on my extensive experience in dealing with holdouts and knowing the principals of the law firm, I knew this would be a time-consuming and expensive settlement.

Not satisfied with the advice of others to turn the building into co-op apartments, I did my own analysis and about a week later I went to Donald and said, "I studied the best use of the building and came to the conclusion that it actually can work as an office building. The experts have been taking the wrong approach and reached the wrong conclusion. You don't have one office building, you have three. They just happen to be on top of each other. You have 400,000 square feet of small office space on the top portion of the building. I don't care what the others say; I think that's rentable at $17 per square foot (which was $2 per square foot *over* the average market rent) because a tenant will have the prestige of renting an entire floor, and a fantastic view of New York harbor."

I also told him that I worked out the financial projections based on his total cost of acquisition and renovation. I concluded that: "If we can take the 400,000 square feet at the top of the building and rent it for $17 per square foot, you'll break even. On the next 300,000 square feet going down, the floors are larger, so even without the views we should still be able to average $17 a square foot in rent. If I can do that, you will make a profit. As for the bottom 300,000 square feet, it doesn't matter if you never rent it as office space. You're in so cheap at $1 per square foot; it won't make any difference what you do with it so long as you can cover the cost of renovation for an occupant."

I outlined my game plan: "First you'll have to do a total makeover of the lobby to make it luxurious, à la Trump style. Second you'll have to renovate the infrastructure to bring it all up to state of the art. This will include the elevators, air conditioning, electrical, and plumbing systems. Third, to be competitive with more modern buildings, all of the latest telecommunication and data systems must be installed and available for tenants. If you agree to do that, I'll do the leasing." Trump replied, "George, make it happen."

Trump borrowed $35 million from Union Labor Life Insurance Company to be used for renovations. They loved the idea of renovating this building because it would put many of their union members back to work. They even stipulated that only union members could be used in construction or renovation. Although the loan was for $35 million, it wasn't nearly enough if we signed tenants and made the improvements that would be required. I told Trump: "If the building is a huge success, it's a terrible loan but if the building bombs, it's a great loan." Nevertheless, based on the past history of failures with the building and the economic climate at that time, it was the only loan Trump could get at that time.

I settled the mechanic liens that existed on the building (almost $1 million) for $60,000. I told all the parties that had the liens, "Look, there's no way you're going to get paid the amount of your claims. But I will give you first crack at renovation work on the building if you give up your liens." Most of them agreed to it, and I gave them an opportunity to bid on the work.

Trump successfully refurbished the building and I started leasing it. The first lease I made was with a major financial firm at a rental of $23 a square foot—far higher than the $17 per square foot I had projected. The building had assumed the mantle of credibility and achieved the recognition of superiority that Trump ownership connotes. As the market rebounded and the building became extremely popular, I rented 400,000 square feet at $24 per square foot on the lower floors to American Express. Later on I rented another 400,000 feet to Continental Casualty Co. at a good rental number. With the influx of tenants Trump replaced the original mortgage with a huge mortgage at a very reasonable interest rate. I'm still involved in leasing and managing it, and today the building, which he bought for $1 million, is worth between $340 and $400 million. It's called the Trump Building and it's a tremendous success.

Insist on Negotiating Directly with the Decision Maker, Not a Representative

Trump's style of negotiation is face-to-face. He rarely lets others negotiate for him. In the Commodore-Hyatt deal described in Chapter 1, Trump negotiated directly with Jay Pritzker, the CEO of the Hyatt Company. But not before spinning his wheels with no results trying to negotiate with Pritzker's underlings. Learn from his early mistake, and as a general rule, don't let others negotiate on your behalf. If you want credibility, do it yourself. Meet important people. Go to the highest level, the decision maker. That was the breakthrough for Trump with 40 Wall Street.

Trump's instincts were that the ground lease owner of 40 Wall Street could not be as bad a businessman as he was portrayed to be. The man obviously would want a good tenant in the property. Yet, the building was in disrepair and barely occupied, the rent wasn't being paid, and Percy Pyne created the impression that the ground lease owner was unreachable and all negotiations had to be done with him. Listening to Pyne, one would believe that, in fact, he was speaking for the owner.

Trump's instinct was that if he wanted to make the deal, he had to get to the owner and talk to him directly, to see whether or not something was being lost in the translation from Percy Pyne. He couldn't believe that a foreign owner of real estate would tolerate this property in its present condition. So he got on a plane and flew to Germany to meet directly with the ground lease owner. There he was able to establish a working relationship of mutual trust that led to successfully negotiating a new ground lease that satisfied both parties. In fact, Trump's relationship with the landowner was so good that while Trump was refurbishing the building (at greater expense than originally planned), Trump asked the owner to waive the rent for a second year. The owner agreed because he was so thrilled with all the work that was going on to make it a first-class building. The waiver saved Trump another $1.5 million in rent. So, by the time Trump had to start paying rent on the ground lease, he had a rental income sufficient to cover all his obligations. As we discussed in Chapter 1, successful, long-term real estate investing is always based on building good personal relationships with the key people involved. The 40 Wall Street deal has a lot to teach small real estate investors about negotiation. Following are explanations of five key principles that Trump used to turn around 40 Wall Street, and how you can use them in your real estate transactions.

PRINCIPLE 1: CREATE THE AURA OF EXCLUSIVITY

One of the most fundamental principles of human nature is that people want something that everyone else wants or no one else has. If you tell someone that a property you own is not for sale there is a good chance they will want it even more. They may even hound you until you name a price. The simple statement that something is a limited edition creates a desire for ownership. For example, the success of any auction sale depends on the number of bidders and the emotional frenzy of a heated bidding environment. Because every parcel of real estate and every building is unique in some way, the exclusivity principle is already at work to drive up the price, but you can get a much higher price, if you can create more exclusivity for your property. Later chapters explain in more detail how Trump does this, but you can create the aura of exclusivity by the way you talk up the features of any property: its location, size, neighborhood, increasing value trends, bargain price, lack of comparable product, or any other selling point that might impress potential tenants or buyers. Embellishment is the order of the day to create excitement and get your target to say "It's a deal."

Using 40 Wall Street as our example, let's look at how Trump created exclusivity. First, he used the variety of floor sizes as a unique selling point. By marketing the building as if it were three separate buildings, one on top of the other, he could offer a tenant a full floor as small as 6,000 square feet and as large as 37,000 square feet. He played up the fact that 40 Wall Street was the only building in the financial area that had such flexibility. The smaller floors at the top of the tower had magnificent views of New York harbor and had the prestige of a full floor for a boutique firm. Visitors would be impressed by seeing a receptionist's desk instead of multiple doors and nameplates as the elevator doors opened. Trump sought out tenants whose space needs were small but who would pay an above market rent to be in a totally refurbished Trump building that catered to their individual needs and gave them great views from all windows.

Second, Trump created exclusivity by insisting that all construction be of the highest quality and workmanship. He redesigned the lobby entrance to create soaring ceiling heights and adorned the floors and ceilings with matching marble slabs from one of the finest quarries in Italy. The heating and cooling equipment and the electrical and plumbing systems were upgraded to those found in new construction. The old elevators were replaced with new cabs and controls that were state of the art.

Third, Trump had the electrical system reconfigured to take advantage of two separate power grids each coming from separate substations. This was used as another exclusive selling point—a breakdown of one substation would not blackout the building. For financial firms on Wall Street, this is a key benefit.

Fourth, Trump applied for and received tax abatements that were available for owners of downtown property willing to undertake renovations. Some of the tax savings could benefit the tenants directly, thus reducing the cost of occupancy. He also was able to convince Con Edison to supply power to the building at a substantial rate reduction which he could pass on to tenants. These exclusive benefits—not offered by other buildings in the area, were incorporated into the marketing campaign. The result was a high rate of occupancy at rental rates much higher per square foot than competitive buildings in the area.

Principle 2: Don't Be Misled by the Aura of Legitimacy

The "aura of legitimacy" traps all who are unaware of the danger it creates. It is the tendency of people to believe things they see in print, or spoken by the media or some other apparently authoritative source. It is insidious and influential in affecting the decision making of all people under its spell. Here are some examples of how it works:

- A document to be reviewed and signed bears the notation: "Standard Form of Contract of Sale" or "Standard Form of Lease" or similar language. This is intended to convey an aura of legitimacy and dissuade buyers or tenants from negotiating terms. But the reality is, there is no such thing as a standard form. It is merely the work product of someone trying to convince the reader that the document is nonnegotiable. *EVERY DOCUMENT IS NEGOTIABLE UNDER APPROPRIATE CIRCUMSTANCES!* You just have to find who has the authority to make revisions and deal directly with that person. If he or she really wants to make a deal with you, you can negotiate the contract or the lease.

- Every new vehicle in a dealer's showroom has an elaborate document prominently displayed on a back window which bears the legend: "Manufacturer's Suggested Retail Price" (the MSRP). It starts with the so-called basic price of a stripped-down vehicle that nobody would actually want to buy. Then it lists, at an inflated, unrealistic price, the value the manufacturer places on every item, which is not included in the basic price. These are characterized as "optional features." This category can include air conditioning system, sound system components, adjustable sideview mirrors, floor mats, a larger engine (which the vehicle really needs), a special paint color, and other features. At the bottom is the grand total. But in reality the MSRP bears little resemblance to the price that the dealer is willing to accept. So when the buyer gets a discount of several thousand dollars off the MSRP he believes he got a "great deal." The aura of legitimacy created by the MSRP gives that illusion.

- A real estate listing by a major real estate broker specified a condominium apartment for sale at a price of "$3.6 million, firm." The word *firm* was inserted in the printed description of the property so that the buyer would come in with an offer close to the asking price. When a friend asked my advice as to how much he should offer for the unit—which sounded like his dream home, I asked: "What offer did you have in mind?" He replied, "Since the seller said $3.6 million *firm*, I intend to offer him $3.4 million." I told him: "Offer $1.8 million." He replied, "The seller will be insulted with such a ridiculous offer and I'll lose the deal." I said, "Try it, and see what happens." He took my advice and eventually bought the apartment for $2.1 million. The aura of legitimacy almost cost him $1.3 million.

A typical instance where the aura of legitimacy can mislead real estate investors is when, for example, reputable real estate brokerage firms turn out a report indicating the current status of the rental or sales market. They have created this aura. They have compiled a survey from a limited sample they have selected; they have arrived at the figures; and they have published the information. And from all this input they arrive at a figure of 13.8 percent vacancy rate for type A office space. Anyone reading this report might conclude, "If the top real estate brokerage firm says that the vacancy rate for my type of building is 13.8 percent and the vacancy rate in my building is only 10 percent, I'm really doing great." But it's just not so. These kinds of market statistics are always averages. They may bear no relation to your particular building. In fact, Trump properties usually sell or rent for much higher than the market average.

When we first started out to lease 40 Wall Street, we interviewed several leasing brokers who wanted the assignment. All were of the opinion that we would never achieve a rental of more than $17 a square foot in the foreseeable future. They gave us a whole bunch of statistics showing the rents at other vacant buildings in the area. But they didn't investigate how 40 Wall Street differed from the norm. We felt 40 was special because of its harbor views and unbroken floor areas, and we were right. The first lease we made on 40 Wall Street with a major financial company was at $23 a square foot. Moreover, the average rent in the building ended up being over $30 a square foot.

Don't be misled by the aura of legitimacy. It is often created by sellers who cloak and tailor their figures with information they picked up from dubious sources to make something appear as gospel. Be skeptical of the expenses and income that are reported on any real estate building, that you are interested in purchasing, and verify all this information for yourself.

Trump versus the Aura of Legitimacy

In the 1990s, New York City helped create an aura of legitimacy for converting downtown office buildings to apartments in the form of tax incentives and other benefits. All types of inducements were offered, including reduced rates for electricity, property tax reductions or abatements, and credits for rehabilitation costs, all of which were designed to reduce the glut of office space and turn it into residential housing. This would give the city increased tax revenue from the converted buildings. Thus, the city created the aura of legitimacy that residential conversion was the way to go. We also had the real estate brokers pointing to an array of statistics that indicated that 40 Wall Street was doomed as office space. If we succumbed to the aura of legitimacy going residential with 40 Wall Street would have been the thing to do.

Smart real estate investors refuse to accept the aura of legitimacy without intensive investigation, so Trump investigated. He gave me the project and told me to make an independent analysis and tell him what to do. I told him that based on my own firsthand research I thought it could work as office space if he used the aura of legitimacy to his benefit. He began an extensive renovation plan to create new vitality and a new image for a building that had suffered in the past.

He put the Trump name on the building creating the aura of superb management and operation. We created brochures showing the fantastic harbor views and the flexibility of various floor sizes. We boasted of state of the art facilities and the availability of the latest in communication systems. We promised quick approvals of lease terms and quick payment of brokerage fees. And in the end, that's how we leased it as exclusive office space at over $30 per square foot when the "experts"—the aura creators—said it could never be leased, not even at $17 per square foot.

How You Can Avoid the Hypnotic Effect of the Aura of Legitimacy

Don't take everything you read or hear from brokers, sellers, buyers, tenants, experts, or see on television as if it were etched in stone. Be willing to dig to confirm the facts behind whatever type of project you get involved with. For instance, say you're interested in purchasing a four-unit apartment building in a certain area. First, you might go to a local real estate broker and make inquiries about vacancy rates in that area. The broker says, "Well, the statistics I have show that the area has a very low vacancy rate of 3.6 percent and rents are high." That's a start, but you can't just take his or her word for it. In addition, you should do your own survey of apartments in your area to find out what, in reality, the vacancy situation really is and what the asking rental rates are. Otherwise, you might make an erroneous investment decision based on an aura of legitimacy that indicates a low vacancy rate. In fact, the market in your immediate neighborhood could be glutted with vacant units available at distressed rents.

How You Can Use the Aura of Legitimacy Principle to Your Benefit

Now that you know the effect the aura of legitimacy has on others, it's easy to make it work for you. Create eye-catching literature with appropriate favorable newspaper articles, reports from apparently authoritative sources and favorable handpicked comparable properties. Create advertisements or media which stress "last available units," "builder's closeout," "final reduction," "special offer," "one of a kind," or something equivalent that will create the aura you desire. Use your imagination but everything must be plausible to be effective.

PRINCIPLE 3: EVERY NEGOTIATION REQUIRES PREPLANNING

In Chapter 1, I described how Donald Trump uses "Ziff's Principle of Least Effort," which states that people will expend the least amount of effort necessary to conclude any transaction. This dovetails perfectly with the power of preplanning in a negotiation. Most people either don't know how to preplan for a negotiation or even if they have the requisite knowledge are too lazy to spend the time doing so. This is always a huge and often a costly mistake. If you can anticipate the questions you may be asked in a negotiation then you can structure the most plausible and favorable responses to them.

At the beginning of a negotiation, what you say and how you say it can be tailored for maximum effect. For example, the ability to give a prompt well-conceived answer to a sensitive question elicits a feeling of satisfaction in the questioner. Although you may have practiced an answer before the question was raised, preplanning permits you to deliver the response with spontaneity as if you just thought of it. You can say: "How about this idea?" or "I just thought of something that might work." The fact that your impromptu manner of thinking is similar to theirs creates an atmosphere of comfort and mutual trust. Preplanning should also include finding newspaper or magazine articles to reinforce any of your positions. Statistics from seemingly reliable sources are also effective and convincing since they convey the "aura of legitimacy."

Real estate investors have a tendency to think that buying or selling real estate is only one negotiation that only involves one round of planning. It's not. It's a series of perhaps hundreds of negotiations at various stages. Each telephone call is a negotiation; each letter is a negotiation; each communication is, in fact, a negotiation. And they all have to be treated separately, so that the end result is what you want. Every time you communicate, for example, with a potential partner, buyer, seller, or anyone else, you need to set aside time to prepare in order to get the response you're looking for.

PRINCIPLE 4: AVOID A QUICK DEAL

If you try to negotiate a quick deal it is a truism that one party will forget something important. Moreover, this will only become apparent after the deal has closed and it's too late to correct the oversight. Overly fast negotiations often leave one party feeling bitter. A quick deal violates many basic negotiating principles and is rarely the right approach. However, in the hands of a skilled, experienced negotiator, rushing a deal can be an awesome weapon to achieve a result that might never happen if the other side spent more time in careful consideration of important factors. Use extreme caution when accelerating the speed of any negotiation. It's usually best to negotiate slowly.

The reason is that satisfaction of the egos on both sides of a negotiation is essential to a mutually agreeable conclusion. Remember that the word negotiation has "EGO" in it. Each participant must feel he has won a number of hard-fought concessions from his adversaries to satisfy his ego that he has done his job well. Here's a good example: I put an ad in the paper to sell my late-model Porsche. It's in great shape, nice year, with low mileage, and with a price of $30,000. It's a great price and a fair deal. You call me up and say I'll give you $25,000 for the Porsche. And I immediately say, "You have a deal." You just bought a $30,000 automobile for $25,000. But are you happy? No! Because, I accepted your offer so fast, you feel that you could have bought it for $20,000. This was a bad negotiation because the buyer isn't happy. If he can, he may try to find a way to back out. The same is true in negotiating over real estate.

Now take the reverse scenario. I put an ad in the paper to sell the same Porsche for $30,000, but this time you phone me and offer $20,000. And I say, "No, the price is $27,000." And you immediately reply with, "Okay, I'll give you the $27,000." Now the question is, am I happy? No! Because you went so fast from $20,000 to $27,000. If I had stuck to my guns you probably would have gone a little higher and paid the $30,000. I got what I wanted, and you got the Porsche for what you were willing to pay, yet neither of us are happy because we didn't spend enough time going through the bargaining process. In a successful negotiation, I have to convince you, the buyer, that you got it for the cheapest price. And you have to convince me that I sold it for the highest price, so that I feel I got the most out of the transaction. All this takes time, haggling, arguing, and discussing to accomplish. It takes extended negotiation.

So if you are negotiating over a piece of property, go through the motions, even though you might already be satisfied with the price and terms. Because unless the other party has satisfied his ego, he is not going to make the deal, or he is going find a reason not to close on the deal. The other party has to be convinced he is making a good deal. The "invested time philosophy" that I discuss in the next section also involves increasing the amount of time spent in pursuit of a final agreement.

How Trump Avoided a Quick Deal

When Trump flew to Germany to meet with the owner of 40 Wall Street, he knew the existing ground lease had to be changed completely to reflect what he had in mind—creating a lease that would permit the flexibility of major renovations, leasing of space, and covering the possibility of a residential use for the building. This meant that he would have to carefully negotiate every point and change all of the provisions of the existing lease. But as a prerequisite to discussing a deal he had to create an environment conducive to success. Trump had to overcome the fact that the building had a long history of failures, bankruptcies, and mismanagement. To make an acceptable deal, he would need to use lots of preparation, relationship building, and showmanship. First he learned everything he could about the German landlord. From his connections with banks that did business in Germany he learned that the landowner was an 80-year-old multimillionaire who also was the patriarch of the Hinneberg family that was well respected and influential in Germany.

Trump assumed that someone of that stature owning a property over 3,000 miles away wanted the benefits of ownership without the headaches and aggravation that came with the renovation, leasing, and operation of a one-million-square-foot building in a distressed area. So Trump had to amass an arsenal of weapons designed to impress. He assembled pictures of the buildings he had built to show the quality and prestige. He was ready to outline his plans for resurrecting 40 Wall Street to the grandeur it had when it was initially built. He had available for display full color renderings showing the difference between the lobby as it presently existed and the lobby after proposed renovation. He had an explanation of how and where he would invest millions of dollars to re-create a building that would make the ground leaseholder proud.

But all this preparation was just the foundation for Trump's initial meeting. The ultimate purpose of that meeting was to find out what Walter Hinneberg really wanted and construct a scenario that would work for both parties. Hinneberg was impressed that someone of Donald Trump's stature would fly to Germany to meet with him and this enabled Trump to establish the atmosphere of mutual trust that was essential to consummation of the deal.

Trump knew that the history of mistrust that Hinneberg endured with prior building operators could only be overcome with the passage of time, relationship building, and constant negotiation to address the concerns of both parties. Instead of trying to sign a quick deal, Trump took almost a year to hammer out the intricate terms of the new ground lease, one of which was a total rent abatement for a period of three years. Both parties were detail oriented and had to expend a great deal of time, energy, and money. But this also meant they were both committed to making the deal work. Without the time investment, the deal probably would have aborted.

Why You Should Avoid a Quick Deal

If you want to buy, sell, or invest in real estate, you must remember that people are willing to spend time with someone who seems genuinely interested in them and what they have to offer. Trying to make a quick deal sends the opposite message to the person you are dealing with. Likewise, it will be much easier for a seller to brush you off, if you are only interested in the selling price of a property, and show no curiosity about the history of the property, or owner's goals, reasons for selling, and so on. The more questions that are asked and answered over extended periods of time in a real estate transaction, the more useful information you will have to bring to the negotiating table. Asking questions and gathering information also cement the impression of a sincere and continued interest Moreover, it is personally gratifying to the seller or the buyer, and personal satisfaction is an essential element in the consummation of any deal. The harder the negotiation and the more time spent, the greater the satisfaction both sides will have over a hard fought victory.

PRINCIPLE 5: THE INVESTED TIME PRINCIPLE

This is related to principle 4, "Avoid a quick deal." The "invested time principle" says that the more time a person has invested in a transaction, the less likelihood he or she's going to give it up. In a negotiation, you can use this to your advantage by getting the other party to spend time on the deal, with reasonable requests for information, a slow, drawn-out negotiation (when appropriate), and so on. Because people hate the idea of having wasted time on something that doesn't work out, after they have spent enough time on something, they'll do everything they can to salvage the transaction. It's very hard for someone to say, "forget the whole thing" and walk away, after putting in a great amount of time and effort.

How Trump Uses It

In the 40 Wall Street deal, Trump had to negotiate an existing ground lease that was a terrible document from his standpoint, but a great document from the owner's point of view. Trump and his attorneys had to negotiate every point, every clause, and every part of it in order to come up with a document that both parties would be willing to sign. That was and had to be a very tedious and time-consuming transaction.

Trump could have said, "I can live with all these unfavorable clauses because they're not critical to making the building a success." But he knew the desirability of building up the invested time of both parties in the deal. It happens naturally when all of the clauses are negotiated separately, continually, and then revised again and again. By doing the negotiation carefully and slowly the lawyers could arrive at language that might be unusual but acceptable to both sides. Of course, it takes a lot of money to pay the fees of the lawyers and the negotiators involved in the drafting of documents. It required many discussions between lawyers and clients to craft solutions to anticipated problems. But everyone involved could say, "We're moving in the right direction. We're constantly revamping and revising but we believe we come out with something both sides can live with." By utilizing the invested time principle, Trump's list of open issues slowly declined and the mutually agreeable solutions increased until there was only one item in dispute between the opposing lawyers. At the last item they each dug in their heels claiming their position was the only one and recommending that the lease not be signed unless the other party gave in. To solve the stalemate Donald called me to intervene and resolve the disputed issue. The issue involved the agreed split of a condemnation award if the property was taken by the government under eminent domain. I told Donald that the likelihood of a governmental taking was remote and giving more money to the owner in that event was a business risk worth taking. He agreed, and that was the end of a long but very successful negotiation.

How You Can Use the Invested Time Philosophy to Your Advantage

Get all people employed by the other side involved in some phase of the negotiation. Get the buyer or seller to review or create financial information and ask them to make projections of income, expenses, cash flow, profits, and tax implications whenever possible. Solicit questions and then give them answers enabling them to rework their calculations. Get the engineering experts to examine the property and report their findings. Have a title search run and relay any problems to the other side. However, never forget that the invested time philosophy could color your decisions as well, if you and your people are the ones putting in an extensive amount of time and effort. Keep the work you and your team do to the minimum necessary and get the other team to expend as much time, money, and energy as you can.

SUMMARY

Consider how a gourmet chef prepares a special dish. The chef starts with one basic ingredient and then blends it with other items and spices designed to enhance the overall flavor to please a discerning guest. Just think of the negotiating principles in this chapter as the basic ingredient and the negotiating techniques in Chapter 4 as the enhancers. I have seen all these principles work wonders in multimillion dollar real estate deals, and I know they can help you work through difficult negotiations with amazing results.

4

HIGH-POWERED REAL ESTATE
NEGOTIATION TECHNIQUES
AND TACTICS

KEY POINTS.

- The basics of negotiation.
- The goals at the start of any negotiation.
- The sources of negotiation power.
- The five characteristics of a skilled negotiator.
- Critical dos and don'ts of successful negotiation.
- P.O.S.T.-time for negotiators.
- Telephone negotiations.
- Using deadlocks, deadlines, and delays to your advantage.
- More tactics and countermeasures.

I HAVE BEEN NEGOTIATING real estate transactions for giants in the industry for 50 years. But when I was a young lawyer I knew very little about negotiation and as a result, I am sure I unwittingly left a lot of my client's chips on the table. Early on, I recognized my own shortcomings and decided to make an intensive study of the field of negotiation. I researched the tricks of the trade from books and from the more experienced lawyers or negotiators who were often my adversaries. When they did something that was effective, I made it part of my style.

Then, after 20 years of experience in real estate negotiations, I started working with Donald Trump, a negotiating genius from whom I learned even more. This chapter is a compilation of techniques I've learned from negotiating over a thousand real estate deals, coupled with Trump's extremely successful variations on the art of negotiating. We have both learned a lot from our association and if you follow the concepts set forth in this chapter and Chapter 3, you will learn much of what I wish I had known when I was a young attorney.

By the way, almost all of the techniques that are discussed in this chapter and the negotiating principles found in Chapter 3 are applicable to the case studies on Trump investments that appear throughout this book. Once you have digested the meat of Chapters 3 and 4, it will be easy for you to spot how Trump and I used these principles and techniques in the investing case studies.

The real estate community is a tough breed to negotiate with. Because each parcel of real estate is unique—its location, views, and topography are but a few of its characteristics. Therefore, each real estate negotiation is also unique. Developers and landlords are often big risk takers and typically shrewd negotiators, whether dealing in small properties or in multimillion dollar properties. But if you follow the guidelines set forth in this chapter you will be able to swim with the "sharks" without becoming their lunch.

THE BASICS OF NEGOTIATION

Although each of us has been negotiating our entire lives, we know little about it and just do what comes naturally. That's a huge mistake! Negotiation is such an important part of life I am constantly amazed at how little time people spend developing a good technique. One of my main purposes in writing this book is to help you improve your understanding of negotiation and develop the skills necessary to achieve success.

What Is Negotiation?

In my negotiation seminars at New York University, I ask my students every year: What is negotiation? The three best answers I've heard are these:

1. It is one aspect of life where there are no governing rules. Lying is not only permitted, it is an accepted practice.
2. It is accepting an available compromise as a substitute for that which you really thought you wanted.
3. It is a journey to an imaginary destination without a road map where all the signposts and directions are intentionally misleading.

Now let me tell you what negotiation is not:

- It is not a science (all the key concepts are abstract).
- It is not a problem which has a right or wrong answer.
- It is not a situation in which winning is everything.
- It is not an event with continuity.

THE GOALS AT THE START OF ANY NEGOTIATION

The ultimate goal of a negotiation, especially a real estate negotiation is to profit from it. But there are several forms of profit. Of course, the first one is monetary, such as a better price or interest rate. But there can be other valuable outcomes to a negotiation, such as acquiring knowledge about a property. More subtly, often the parties in a transaction also have the unconscious goal of obtaining satisfaction from a negotiation and feeling good about the outcome, or at least not losing face. This is another form of "profit" that you want your opponent to feel they have earned.

However, at the beginning of a negotiation, real estate investors (or anyone in a negotiation) should focus on the following immediate goals:

- *Learn the other side's position.* If we learn what the other parties want we can attempt to structure a transaction that meets their needs. There is always a reason or reasons why the other side is willing to consider doing a deal. If you "find the story" of what they really want and think is important, you can address their concerns.
- *Understand the constraints surrounding the transaction.* Every transaction has some controlling factors such as a time frame, competing offers, tax implications, or required approvals. If you learn what they are you can use them to your advantage.

- *Define "fair and reasonable."* What these words mean to each negotiating party may be very different. Understanding that there is a difference in what each side considers "fair and reasonable" is necessary before you can start to reduce the gap in perception between the two sides.
- *Assess "your side."* The personality, knowledge, and skills of the people on your team are equally important to know.
- *Assess the "other side."* It is essential to know the personalities, knowledge, and desires of your opponents. Are they sophisticated, or abrasive, or people you can be comfortable negotiating with? If you think they are untrustworthy, you should run for the nearest exit! One thing that should be perfectly clear in negotiating: There is no way you can ever protect yourself against a thief. No legal document can protect you. Nothing can. If you get involved with someone who is a thief, you're in big trouble.

Do You Really Want to Do Business with These People?

After you've researched and digested all the available information about the parties you're dealing with in a real estate transaction, it's time to trust your instincts. Everyone develops instinctive reactions as a result of prior learning experiences, and when your instincts prove right in a situation, you gradually begin to learn to trust them in the future. When an instinct proves wrong, you quickly learn to abandon it. The result of this sorting process is the creation of a set of instincts that your experience tells you can be trusted.

Your instincts are usually pretty close to being right, especially once you have developed a style of negotiation you are comfortable with. If the deal doesn't feel right; if you instinctively feel like you're dealing with someone who's shady, don't deal with them. You may never be able to prove it, but it is your instinct that has triggered a response. And usually your instincts are right because you have developed them over a long period of time. If you think the deal is too good to be true, it probably is. Or, if you think the person you're getting involved with is someone who seems to remind you of the snake oil salesman in old movies and is prone to exaggerate, or you can't trust what they say, then don't get involved with them.

Here's an example I often use that confirms the value of instinct. You're walking down the sidewalk and farther down you see a group of men. They appear to be a gang of rowdy teenage boys. Instinctively you sense trouble, they're doing something that you sense could become a problem or be a source of danger. So, instinctively you cross the street and begin walking on the other side. And you do this because of something that has happened in your past that tells you instinctively what to do.

Also, if someone comes across as a straight shooter but you feel they're just too good to be true—you shouldn't do business with them. Rely on your gut feeling. I'm not saying you shouldn't trust people, but investigation is a necessity. I will take at face value anything that is said by somebody whom I think I can completely trust, but I'll check everything out later. In fact, I always start out with a lot of assumptions about a real estate deal or people involved in a deal, but I assume that every assumption is wrong. Then I'm surprised when an assumption proves right. I always assume that I am dealing with a trustworthy individual. But I investigate and do a background check to verify the validity of my assumption. Then I'll be satisfied that my assumption was right.

However, I may end up with a situation where I checked this person out and he seemed trustworthy, but along the way he does something that changes my opinion. What should you do when you're dealing with partners you feel you can't trust? Get out! That trust can never be reinstated. Never! Your partner says he'll never do it again, but once the trust has been breached, it can never be corrected. It's like the husband who cheats on his wife, and he says "Honey, I'll never do it again." The wife is crazy if she believes him!

SOURCES OF NEGOTIATING POWER

Negotiating power is the ability and resources to influence others. Some subtle forms of negotiating power include:

- *Good record keeping.* Having good records favors the party who has them when there is a disagreement about what or when something was said. He who has better records and better notes wins the argument about what was said when, and who promised to do what.
- *Preprinted forms.* These favor the party supplying them. For example, if a contract is titled "Standard Purchase Agreement" people assume it's nonnegotiable.
- *Company policy.* The mere statement: "That's our company policy" usually puts an end to many disputes.
- *Knowledge.* Revealing that you have a lot of knowledge or information about a transaction can intimidate the other side so they will ask for fewer concessions. Often people think: "He's too smart for me to try to get this concession."
- *The willingness to take risks.* Assume I have tossed a coin 50 times and each time it came up heads. So I say to you: "I'll give you 10 to 1 odds that it will come up heads again." Now there's a bet you would be inclined to take since you know the real odds are 50–50. Assume that your entire fortune at that time is $100,000 and I say: "It's my million against your $100,000, okay?" Somehow you start thinking: "With my fortune on the line, it'll

probably come up heads again, and I'll lose everything." Your willingness to take a risk has entered the negotiating arena and colored your decision.

- *Time.* Time is the ultimate negotiating power. Every real estate transaction has a time frame within which the parties must work if they want to make a deal. He who controls the timing controls the deal.

FIVE CHARACTERISTICS OF A SKILLED NEGOTIATOR

A renowned researcher in the field of negotiation conducted a survey in which CEOs of major corporations were asked to rate, in order of importance, the requisite qualities of people they would utilize to negotiate on their behalf. Even though I had developed my own ideas, their choices surprised me. Here they are:

1. *Personality.* They believed that a good personality was more important than knowledge. (That shocked me.)
2. *Knowledge of the subject matter.* I thought that would have been #1!
3. *Ability to organize information.* This speaks volumes for the importance CEOs placed on good work habits such as record-keeping and efficient filing and retrieval systems.
4. *Knowledge of human nature.* Wouldn't you think this would have a higher ranking?
5. *Ability to find and exploit weaknesses.* CEOs were interested in utilizing people who had the brainpower and mental agility to probe the other side without setting off any warning bells, and then use the information gained to their advantage.

The next section of this chapter describes how you can develop these five negotiation skills that CEOs value most highly.

Improve Your Personality

Be a "nice person" to deal with. Be friendly. Make others feel "comfortable" in talking and dealing with you. This is essential. If people like you they'll go all out to please you. Look for common ground to establish a good rapport with the other side. Find a common theme for discussion. Look around their offices or desks. If they're interested in sports—talk sports. Look for family pictures and ask questions about them. "Is that your grandchild? She looks like a tomboy, is she? How many grandchildren do you have? How many boys? Do you see them often?" The greater interest you show in them, the more you engender a "warm and cozy" feeling.

Exhibiting a good sense of humor is usually an excellent ice-breaker, but stay clear of anything that might be considered offensive.

Let it be known that you are a *deal maker*, not a *deal breaker*. Convince the other side of your sincerity and desire to reach a mutually amicable conclusion.

Learn flexibility. In negotiation, you rarely get exactly what you want. Getting close or achieving an acceptable alternate is equivalent to total victory.

Establish a reputation of trustworthiness. If you promise to call, do so. If you say, "I'll get you that information," get it. Remember there is a severe discount factor for lack of trust. You can never quantify the amount of the discount. No one ever asks for a pound of friendship or a bucket of integrity but they are always willing to pay (in the form of granting concessions) if you deliver friendship and integrity in the negotiation process.

Display Knowledge of the Subject Matter

An interesting phenomenon I mentioned earlier in this chapter is that if you convince your adversaries that you have extensive knowledge—even though you really don't, you may win many points when your adversaries overestimate how savvy you really are. They may abandon a negotiation strategy thinking: "He's too smart for that to work." The kind of knowledge you want to display to your adversary in a negotiation falls into two categories:

1. *Actual knowledge.* This is the knowledge obtained by one's own private experiences and education. You can easily increase your store of knowledge by talking to outside professionals prior to and during negotiations. Never be afraid or shy to ask questions from someone in the know. The only stupid question is the one you didn't ask! Having discussions with experts or people on your side is essential to obtaining the information you need to shape your approach to any upcoming negotiation.

2. *Apparent knowledge.* This is the broad, or even superficial information that a negotiator exhibits when discussing a particular subject. When coupled with a smooth authoritative delivery it can prove very effective. It may involve knowledge that the negotiator gained from comparable negotiations with comparable adversaries in comparable situations. For example, if you're dealing with a loan officer from a new bank and you've dealt with loan officers from other banks, you can assume that the same corporate procedures and mentality will be found. Displaying your knowledge of loan procedures to the new loan officer will make the officer less likely to pad the bank's fee, and more likely to make the adjustments you ask for.

Organize Your Information: Donald Trump's Spiral Notebook and Other Tools

If you want to develop this highly desirable characteristic it is essential that you develop a work habit and an infallible method of filing information for *immediate* retrieval. You will find this a lifesaver when you're under stress. I suggest you use a simple spiral notebook, not a loose leaf one where pages are removable. If you look at Donald Trump's desk you will see his spiral notebook in which he chronicles all his telephone calls and things to do. If it's an important work habit for him, why not for you? Stop writing notes, telephone numbers, or other information on the back of envelopes or on those treacherous little colored tags that stick to anything and tend to disappear when you try to find them.

Another great technique is creating a checklist of open issues, which is subject to constant revision. As you get more involved in real estate you will find that one deal looks like many others and it becomes difficult, if not impossible, to keep the status of negotiations separate. An up-to-date checklist helps immensely.

Another valuable tool is a "we-they list" of the different positions taken by each of the parties. This will clarify the *zone of uncertainty* mentioned earlier. It helps tremendously to write down the key facts about which you and the other party have fundamentally different and conflicting perceptions and beliefs. These need to be faced and attacked to enable the transaction to reach a mutually acceptable conclusion.

I supplement this "we-they list" with a "wish list" in which I jot down how I would like to resolve certain issues, or get the other side to accept a new concept. This is a valuable aid because it forces me to think of possible solutions and scenarios to make them a reality.

Somewhere in the midst of negotiation, I also recommend you prepare a scorecard in which you name all of the players, identify their roles in the transaction, and evaluate their plusses and minuses, to help you understand what each person wants, what you can offer them, and how they could help or hurt your position in the negotiation.

These tips are not meant to be all-inclusive but they constitute a strong foundation on which your own unique style of organizing information can be built.

Improve Your Knowledge of Human Nature

Many of the following basic truths may seem obvious and simplistic to you but I doubt you have spent a substantial amount of time analyzing the impact they have on the outcome of negotiations. Researchers in the field of negotiation have done extensive, comprehensive experiments to prove the validity of these concepts. I cannot stress too strongly that the time you spend making them part of your base of knowledge is time well spent. It will be extremely helpful in your future negotiations.

- *Create exclusivity.* I mentioned this in Chapter 3 but it's so important it warrants repeating: People want what they can't have or somebody else wants. If someone announces: "That's not for sale at any price" everyone thinks that there must be some price at which it can be bought. This concept is found at the heart of all auctions. The more bidders for an item, the higher the bids and the more spirited the bidders.
- *People become overwhelmed when they are faced with too many decisions.* Once you accept this fact you can easily understand why it is best to use a "little at a time" approach. Just imagine that you want someone to swallow a pill the size of a golf ball. If you tried to give it to him at one time, he would choke on it. If, however, you cut the pill up into little pieces and gave it to him at various intervals, he would swallow the entire pill and never realize what you made him do.
- *The "aura of legitimacy" phenomena.* I discussed this extremely important topic in Chapter 3. If you're still unclear about its power to work for you or against you, I suggest you reread that chapter.
- *Satisfaction.* Everyone in a negotiating situation has a "need for satisfaction." People want to believe that they have conducted a successful negotiation and have won hard fought concessions

from you. To satisfy that need you must learn to hold back. Be stingy with your concessions even though they may be of little importance to you, the fact that the other side got you to give in on an item is considered a win for them. Because winning a hard fought issue, which was the subject of protracted negotiation, creates the feeling of deep self satisfaction in the winner it is important for you to leave time in the negotiation for this to happen. Learn to cater to the needs of individuals. Tell them how they out-negotiated you and drove such a hard bargain. Tell them they got an unbelievable price and you don't know how they did it. Everyone likes to be flattered. Do it, even if you feel that you might choke on the words.

- *People have an innate fear of superiority in others.* While it's important to display your knowledge of the subject matter in a negotiation, you don't want to appear so smart that people are afraid to deal with you.

  In recognition of this you must sometimes adopt the principle that "dumb" is "smart." Sol Goldman who will be discussed later was a multimillionaire with a humble background as a grocery vendor. Notwithstanding his lack of formal education, he had one of the sharpest minds I ever encountered. He was a brilliant negotiator who played a major role in my successful growth as a negotiator. He could remember anything and everything about any piece of real estate or anyone in the real estate arena. In any negotiation the other parties never had a clue as to the extent of his proficiency. If someone said something he needed time to consider, he'd say, "You people are much smarter than I am. Could you please give me a simpler explanation that my small mind can understand?" He knew full well what was being proposed as well as what his answer might be. But, often the simplified explanation was more attackable than the initial one, and if that was true he would respond to that one. His delay in responding also gave him the time to sharpen his response and then deliver it as if he were a local yokel shooting from the hip without considering the depth of the subject matter. When Sol Goldman died in 1987, his real estate holdings were appraised at over $700 million and reputed to be second in size only to the holdings of New York City. Not bad for someone who gave the appearance of being dumb.

- *Ziff's Principle of Least Effort.* As I mentioned in Chapter 1, Ziff was a researcher who concluded that in any negotiation people will expend the least amount of effort to arrive at a result. You can use this principle to your advantage by agreeing to do all the work that the other side really doesn't want to do. Tell the other side that you know how busy they are and you will take a load off of them by doing much of the menial work. Besides appearing to be helpful, if you are the party who originates and controls the documentation and preparation of financial information relating to any transaction you have a huge edge. You know what you put in the documentation and what you left out. The reader has a tendency to be trapped by the written word and concentrates on what he sees, not what he doesn't see. Let Ziff's findings work for you.

- *Everyone loves a "freebie."* This principle is the cornerstone of many successful marketing and sales strategies. "Buy one get one free." "If you take advantage of this special offer, we'll send you another gizmo absolutely free." "Buy today and we'll pay the shipping charges." The list is endless but it works. Try to come up with something you are willing to throw into the deal without charge and that minor inducement might win the day.

- *People believe in the "one good turn theory."* "One hand washes the other" and "One good turn deserves another" are considered by most people to be the fair way of doing business. I tend to agree with that bit of philosophy. However, it doesn't mean that an equal exchange is required, just that there be a quid pro quo. There's nothing that says your "quid" must have the same value as their "quo." Embrace the concept but slant the exchange in your favor. Others will be so enthralled by your fairness that they forget to weigh the respective benefits of the items exchanged.

- *Everyone is influenced by the power of a simple solution.* Somehow "Let's split the difference" seems only fair to most people. Throw it out as a solution if it's in your interest to do so, but if it's offered to you, don't accept it if you think it's not fair to you. "Let's discuss this later" is an easy way to avoid locking horns over an issue where feelings run high.

- *People appreciate a person who can say, "I made a mistake."* Suppose you made an offer to purchase a building for $200,000 and the offer was accepted. After further consideration, you told the seller that the cost of needed repairs was much higher than you thought and you wanted to reduce the purchase price by $40,000 If the seller accuses you of bad faith and reneging on your agreement just say, "I'm terribly sorry but I made an honest mistake and you wouldn't take advantage of that, would you?" That admission may get you part or all of the $40,000 discount you asked for.

- *Most people are stricken by the "deadline syndrome."* Just before time runs out is the most effective time to win your objective. When your opponent is facing a deadline such as, "I have to report to my boss by 3 P.M. today" closing open issues happens quickly after 2:45 P.M. Find out what the other party's deadline is, wait until the last minute to resolve key issues, then see the favorable result you get.

- *People want their "invested time" to pay off for them.* I discussed how the "invested time" principle works in Chapter 3. Donald

Trump and I have used it to achieve results that we originally thought were not attainable.

Finding and Exploiting Weaknesses

Information is power in a negotiation. I have to derive information from you, and to do that, I have to ask you a lot of questions. If I said to you, "Are you really in such a bind that you have to move out of your property in the next few weeks?" You're never going to tell me yes, because that's going to hurt your negotiation posture. So instead, you say "I want to move in by the end of the year." And I respond by saying, "I don't know if that's possible, suppose I gave it to you three months later?" You reply, "I can't use it three months later, I have to use it now." Without you realizing it, you just told me you're in a bind. All I did was throw out an alternative, and you said that "I couldn't live with the alternative." Which effectively got me the answer to my question.

Another indirect question might be, "What if instead of us paying all cash, you take back a mortgage for $25,000?" If the reply is, "I really need the cash to pay off the debt to my bank." Guess what—you've discovered a weakness that you may be able to capitalize on. Sometimes a timing question elicits a helpful response. You pose the following question, "Would you be upset if I extended the lease commencement date by three months?" The answer, "I can't do that, my present lease expires in 60 days." You have just gained valuable information without asking a direct question which might not be answered truthfully.

In another situation I might say, "Why do you want to sell it now?" "Well, the truth is I'm not feeling well." Now I found out why he's selling. Also, I could ask a seller, "Have you heard about this or that" and he says no. Now I've got a feeling if they're in tune with the market. Again, information is power in a negotiation.

One of the things that can significantly weaken the other side's position is when they have rejected your offer to take a better offer, but that falls through and they come back to you. In a case like that, you can press your advantage, as I once did when negotiating the purchase of a radio station, WGLI on Long Island in the late 1960s. The seller initially wanted $500,000 all cash. My brother-in-law and I were partners and we offered $450,000—$50,000 in cash and a $400,000 mortgage. Their lawyer rejected the offer and said "we have an all-cash offer of $500,000, which we're taking." A month later, the same lawyer called me and said, "the other deal fell through, we will accept your offer." Well now he's in my ballpark! I said, "What offer?" He said, "Well, you said you'd pay $450,000 with terms." I replied, "Yes, but unfortunately that was a month ago. We have since invested the bulk of our money in several other projects. But if you're willing to recast the deal, we will think it over." I went to my brother-in-law and said I think they'd accept $400,000 with $100,000 down and the balance in a 4 percent mortgage. "Go ahead," he said. So I made the offer, and they accepted it! That's how I got into the radio business, on extremely good terms—I exploited the seller's weakness.

BY GEORGE . . . THE SOL GOLDMAN
NEGOTIATING STYLE

Learn which techniques are most effective with the other side. If they hate paperwork, barrage them with paper. If they can't tolerate long discussions, drag them out. If they are intimidated by an angry outburst, display your anger when it is appropriate to do so. Sol Goldman once used this tactic very effectively in a negotiation I participated in before I joined the Trump Organization. Goldman wanted to buy a building, and he was willing to pay $15 million, all cash. (Goldman was a multimillionaire who became one of the richest men in America, and he had a lot of available cash on hand.)

Goldman initiated the negotiations by asking the seller, "How much do you want for the building?" The seller said, "$15 million, all cash." Goldman replied in a high-pitched screech, "W H A T!?"

Well, this was the price Goldman was willing to pay, and the seller was willing to take. But Goldman was so indignant in the way he said "WHAT?" The seller responded by saying, "Well maybe we can take a little less; how about $14 million, all cash." Goldman says again with the same high-pitched screech, "WHAT?! ALL CASH. YOU WANT ALL CASH?!"

The seller then said, "Well, maybe we can talk terms."

Now Sol Goldman never tipped his hand—he never said anything substantial—while all this was going on. All he said was "WHAT?!" at four different times. The seller thought he was so indignant, so insulted, that Goldman ended up buying the building for $12 million with terms! And all he said was "WHAT!"

You have to understand that as a young lawyer, working for Sol Goldman, I was ready to grab the seller's first offer, since I knew my client was ready to pay it. Instead, Goldman would negotiate without making a single counteroffer. He never said, "All I want to pay is $12 million." All he ever said was "WHAT?" "WHAT?" "WHAT?" "WHAT?"

Later on, Goldman inquired, "What's the interest rate on the mortgage?" And the seller replied, "8 percent."

Goldman again replied with another indignant and ear-piercing "WHAT, 8 PERCENT?!"

The whole tone of the entire negotiation made the seller feel that he was insulting my client. It ended up having an unbelievable result.

Later, in another negotiation with Goldman, he was ready to sell a building for $20 million. An interested buyer came along and offered him $20 million. But Goldman said, "You've got to do better than that."

So the other side replied, "Well, how about $22 million."

(Continued)

Again, Goldman replied, "You've got to do better than that."

Now Goldman had already made $2 million and he was willing to accept $20 million, but just by saying "You've got to do better than that," made the other side feel that they had to. Otherwise, they thought Goldman wouldn't make the deal. It was just a ploy—which worked! In this example, Goldman succeeded in a negotiation by giving away no information.

CRITICAL DOS AND DON'TS OF SUCCESSFUL NEGOTIATION

The negotiation principles and techniques I'm describing are powerful, but they won't all work for you. It's important to adopt your own style of negotiating. Each person has a unique personality and method of negotiating. If you try to simply copy someone else, people sense that your trying to hide the truth of who or what you are. This will result in a quick turnoff because they feel you cannot be trusted.

- *Don't* talk about your weaknesses at any time or in front of anyone. Be sure to muzzle everyone on your side. Many deals are blown by nonnegotiators who couldn't keep their mouths shut.
- *Don't* believe in the "bogey" theory. Very often in real estate deals you will be told, "Look if you don't want the deal I have two others who do." Another variation is, "I've got a better price from someone else." Don't give those statements any credence. If there were any truth to the claim, they wouldn't be dealing with you, but instead they would be pursuing the other, better deal.

- *Don't* trust your assumptions. If you start with the belief that all your assumptions and estimates are wrong, you're never disappointed but you feel good when you find out some of them were right.
- *Don't* assume the other side knows what you know. Find out what they know during the course of negotiations.
- *Don't* accept any offer right away. Hold back. Remember that the other side wants a sense of "satisfaction" out of the negotiation. Don't make things too easy for them or they will wonder how much money they left on the table.
- *Do* be indecisive to drag out the negotiation. (Remember creating a "time investment" by the other side is helpful in obtaining a satisfactory conclusion.)
- *Don't* do quick negotiations. In quick negotiations, one side gets an inferior deal. The exception is when you are clearly more skilled and more prepared than the other side. Skilled and well prepared wins in quick negotiations.
- *Don't* use all the power you possess. Always leave the door open for future dealings. This is a critical necessity in any long-term relationship.
- *Don't* forget that there's no right price for the wrong property.

P.O.S.T.-Time for Negotiators

Negotiation is like a horse race, but the secret to winning is running a smart race. Before you go into any negotiation think of each key meeting with the other party as your "post time." For example, at your first meeting, you know little or nothing about the opposition and what the outcome will be. Use the P.O.S.T. acronym to prepare for your post time:

P—Stands for the persons attending the negotiation. Learn who they are and their functions. Never negotiate if there are unidentified people present. Find out who they are and what role they will play in the deal. Learn who is decision maker for each element under discussion.

O—Stands for the objective you wish to accomplish at the meeting you are attending. Figure this out before you start any meeting. Your objective must be measurable by the end of the negotiation meeting to be useful. If you believe your objective in an initial meeting is to finalize a deal, you're aiming at the wrong target. A better objective is, "Let's see if the seller is someone I want to do business with." That's a clear target, easy to measure.

S—Stands for the strategy you intend to use in the negotiation. This is your game plan or overall approach that you intend to take. The strategy will dictate who talks on what topics, who answers specific questions raised at any time, and who makes notes of what was discussed and what the result was of such discussion.

T—Stands for tactics to be used. This is a subcategory of strategy. It is the "nuts and bolts" to be used for the implementation of the game plan. For example you might say, "We're going to use the good guy-bad guy approach. Sam, I want you to play the tough guy and appear to be hard-nosed and inflexible. I'll play the good guy and act as a mediator." How you script the negotiation is up to you but don't go into one without knowing what you plan to say or do. However, your tactics should differ if there is a long-term versus a short-term relationship being created. Long-term relationships must be nurtured with an abundance of tender, loving care. You can be more aggressive in negotiations that involve short-term relationships.

Post-Negotiation Review

It is extremely important that a review be done as soon as possible after each negotiation. This is an absolute must! At the review, the following questions should be asked and answered:

Were the objectives achieved? If not, why not?

What was good and what was bad in the negotiation?

What changes should we make to our prior assumptions?

What about next time? Was a schedule set? Were there assigned tasks to be done? If so, who has to do them and when?

After all these questions have been answered make appropriate notes and put them in your infallible file system for immediate retrieval when necessary.

TELEPHONE NEGOTIATIONS

Telephones are part of every negotiation, but telephone negotiations have advantages and disadvantages. The main advantage is time savings. Telephone negotiations can be easily conducted at a specific time acceptable to all parties. Telephone negotiations are convenient and with the advent of cell phones, calls can be made to or from almost anywhere. Conference calls are also valuable for bringing together many interested parties regardless of where they are located. Despite these obvious advantages the telephone has some distinct drawbacks.

Telephone Traps You Should Know

- One party will often forget something in a telephone negotiation, because both sides tend to prepare less for a telephone negotiation. The only question is how important the forgotten item is.

- You lose the chance to read facial expressions and body language. This can be significant, especially early on in a negotiation.

- One party to the call is always unprepared unless the call was scheduled in advance, and there was a specific understanding of what would be discussed. You should never be the one unprepared.

- Interruptions are deadly. Anything that interferes with one's chain of thought can lead to disaster.

- During a telephone negotiation you never know who may be listening and why they're listening. Even if you ask, "Is anyone else on this line?" you may not get a truthful answer.

- During a telephone call you cannot examine any documentation which is referred to by the other party. They may say, "I have statistics which show your building is overpriced." You can't refute what you cannot see.

- In telephone negotiations there is always a tendency toward resolution. Before the parties hang up they like to feel they have accomplished something, usually some type of agreement on one or more points.

The key to mastering telephone negotiations is learning to listen! When you answer the call, just ask the caller, "What's the purpose of this call?" Then relax and just listen carefully. If you don't talk the other side must talk or there is an awkward silence that people find intolerable. After you have listened and gotten all the information you wanted, tell the caller that you will call him or her back. This gives you the time necessary to craft a proper reply.

When you call back, do it from a quiet place at a good time, to minimize the chance of interruptions. Have all pertinent material you need readily available before you participate in a telephone negotiation. Helpful tools include a checklist which serves as an agenda, and a calculator in case it's needed. Take good notes during the conversation and put them in your spiral notebook. When the call is over, see that the notes go into the appropriate file. It's a good policy to confirm the conversation and the agreements reached by a follow-up letter, fax, or e-mail.

Using Deadlocks, Deadlines, and Delays to Your Advantage

Deadlocks

When both parties have reached an impasse (i.e., a deadlock), ask yourself if a deadlock is appropriate at this time and on this issue. A deadlock usually results from constraints placed on negotiators by someone on their own side. If you think you have reached a genuine deadlock, and you opt to leave the negotiation, be pleasant. Smile when you walk out and say something like, "I'd really like to buy your property but your price is not realistic." Always leave the door open for "face saving" (e.g., "I'll give it some thought.").

If one party welcomes a deadlock, that party has a distinct advantage. A deadlock does not necessarily represent the end of a negotiation, or even a failure, but most people view it as such. In many cases you will learn of the availability of other concessions from the other side, if you let a negotiation reach a deadlock on an issue.

Big organizations dread a deadlock because they view a deadlock as failure. But savvy real estate investors know that deadlocks are not failures and can always be broken. This gives you an advantage when dealing with a big organization.

In many cases, you should welcome a deadlock because it clearly shows your determination to the other side. A deadlock also tests the other parties' determination. If they say, "That's something I refuse to accept and I'm leaving," see if they actually go out and stay out. Often if you call their bluff, they will retreat and accept your position or suggest an alternative. Try to orchestrate a way for them to gracefully come back to the table and accept your position or suggest an alternative, without losing face. If the other side accepts a deadlock it proves to you and your side that "it's the end of the road" on that issue, though not necessarily the whole deal.

Breaking Deadlocks

One way to break a deadlock is simply to change the subject that caused the deadlock and shift to other areas. The issue may still be unresolved but if agreement is reached on other items the mood may be changed and the deadlock issue can be revisited in a more amicable environment.

Another way to break a deadlock is to go "off the record" and try to open an avenue of resolution through a different person, perhaps at a different level in the opposing party's organization. Or you can offer to get the opinion of a mutually respected third party.

If you do intend to break a deadlock by caving in, you should at least insist on getting a minor concession in an ancillary area to maintain a degree of credibility.

Using Deadlines to Your Advantage

Most people wait until the last minute to resolve open issues in a negotiation. An interesting experiment was undertaken by a noted researcher in the field of negotiation. He assembled a group of

100 negotiators with varied degrees of skill to participate in a mock negotiation. The participants were divided into two groups on opposite sides of the following imaginary situation. A large pharmaceutical company had developed a drug, which they publicized as having some minor side effects such as occasional dizziness or headaches, but they also knew that it could lead to possible blindness or serious loss of sight.

People were suing for serious injuries suffered. The negotiators were split into teams of two, one person representing the drug company and the other person representing the claimant. They had to reach a settlement within 60 minutes or a deadlock would be declared and negotiation cease. A bell would sound every 10 minutes and an announcement made specifying the time remaining. During the last 10 minutes the bells and announcements sounded every minute. The experiment disclosed that over 90 percent of the claims were settled in the last 5 minutes. The lesson for real estate investors is, "plan on doing the real intensive negotiation just before a deadline expires."

The worst deadlines that have to be faced are those that affect your side. As the deadline approaches, the other side has the time to remain flexible but your hand is quickly being forced to make a deal, under potentially unfavorable terms.

It is important to know which deadlines are real and which are fictitious. If someone says, "I must have your answer by Friday." Tell them you have to check things out and won't have the answer until the following Wednesday. If they say, "Okay," you know the deadline was not really a deadline. If they have a plausible explanation for the Friday deadline—it's real.

Delays

It is a fact that every transaction will meander unless there is a compelling reason to consummate it or kill it. If you want to speed things up, take control by setting acceptable time frames and insisting that they are met. If you take the time to coordinate the schedules of all necessary participants you can avoid unforeseen delays.

Try to establish as many "parallel tracks" as possible (i.e., lots of people working on different parts of the transaction in the same time period). To the extent that the other side has multiple people working on the transaction (the broker, lawyer, inspector, etc.) it adds to their "invested time" account.

Murphy was right when one of his laws stated that everything takes longer than you think. Unless a delay works in your favor, take the necessary steps to keep the transaction moving at a reasonable pace consistent with the size and complexity of the deal.

MORE TACTICS AND COUNTERMEASURES

Take it or leave it. That statement is considered to be fighting words, and the recipient of that ultimatum is usually seriously offended by it. To minimize the adverse effect try to tone it down by saying, "I have other offers" or "Here's a comparable building at a much lower price." Try to leave yourself a way out for face saving should you decide to come back at a later date. The good things to be said about using "take it or leave it" are that it shortens negotiations and shows the resolve of the party taking that stand. The countermeasure to "take it or leave it" is to change the parameters of the discussion. Try to look for other areas that need further dialogue which may help reduce the tension that the ultimatum created and ultimately eliminate it as a factor.

You've Got to Do Better Than That (aka "The Crunch"). If you say "You've got to do better than that" to someone their normal reaction is to modify their position in your favor. If you say it again, they'll probably go further. Note that you never indicate that you will accept their modified position. You're just fishing to see if there's a better deal available. The countermeasure is simple, just say "I already have offered a fair deal, there's no reason for me to make it better for you."

The Change of Pace. This tactic involves changing a cooperative atmosphere into a negative or somewhat hostile environment or vice versa. This can be an effective tactic if you're intent on making the deal and are afraid that the other side is backing off. If you stirred things up, you can always retreat and appear friendly by doing so. If the other side changes the negotiating environment for the worse, the effective countermeasure for you is to reaffirm your previous assumptions and create a "bogey." As an illustration, you could say, "After all we've been through I thought you really wanted to make this deal. Do you? If not, I have another piece of real estate I'm ready to buy."

5

THE TRUMP TOUCH

*Create "Sizzle," Glamour, and Prestige to Get
Higher-Than-Market Prices for Your Properties*

KEY POINTS

- Be distinctive; add "sizzle" to your property.
- Give your customers the ultimate in perceived quality.
- Understand your buyers' and tenants' lifestyles.
- Know what your customers will pay extra for and what they won't.

A KEY PART OF Trump's real estate investing philosophy is his passion to ensure that whatever he is building or renovating is the epitome of its type in terms of quality, prestige, beauty, workmanship, and meticulous detail. The creation of perfection is why, in 2003, nine out of the top ten highest selling condominium residences in New York City were in buildings built by Trump. Trump properties consistently command a high premium over comparably located and comparable sized properties because of the special exciting features that embody what the industry recognizes as "the Trump Touch." If you want willing buyers to pay higher prices for your real estate, you must include unusual, dazzling features that will appeal to buyers or tenants on several emotional levels. Trump Tower on 5th Avenue is a prime example of how this kind of "sizzle" can increase the value of a property far beyond the cost of creating the sizzle. In the following case study, you'll learn techniques that Trump uses to get the highest prices in the market for anything he sells or rents. I'll also show you how you can apply the same techniques, on a smaller scale, to your own real estate investments.

INVESTING CASE STUDY

TRUMP TOWER ON 5TH AVENUE

Imagine yourself in midtown Manhattan walking down the most fashionable part of 5th Avenue. When you get to 56th Street your breath is taken away by a towering, modern, distinctive building with a unique jagged facade of black glass. As you look up, your eye catches a grove of 16 full-size trees planted on six floors of terraces the lowest of which is 50 feet above the level of the sidewalk. Upon entering the 68-story tower, you are flanked by attractive show windows of renowned retail stores. You marvel at the highly polished floor of exquisitely matched marble slabs which lead into the spacious high-ceiling tree-lined lobby that ends at the huge seven-story atrium. Tumbling down the far wall of the atrium is a 100-foot waterfall against a marble wall that is topped by a large angled skylight that illuminates everything below. The lower level of the atrium houses two fine eating places, one of which is a tempting elaborate buffet and the other has starched white tablecloths and elegant décor. Both facilities have excellent food prepared by a master chef. Surrounding all of the furnishings, you notice the perfectly matched marble-lined walls and the attention to detail this interior space was given. Highly polished brass is everywhere. Off to the left of the main entrance is a bank of elevators housed in mirror-finish brass doors. As you approach the elevators, a well-dressed security man asks you whom you are visiting. After receiving the approval of the party you intend to visit, you are permitted to enter the high-speed mirrored elevators to take you to your desired floor.

This is how people experience the lobby and office portion of Trump Tower for the first time. It is dazzling, and proves Trump is a master at creating awe-inspiring buildings. The residential portion of the building is a world unto itself. It has its own private entrance on 56th Street with 24-hour doorman and concierge service. The reception desk is staffed by uniformed personnel who are trained to recognize all residents and screen all visitors. Once visitors are cleared, they are permitted to enter one of the immaculately clean elevators where a uniformed operator inquires as to their destination and whisks them to it.

Because magnificent views command higher prices, Trump designed the building so that the residential portion of Trump Tower,

Trump Tower on 5th Avenue

which contains luxury condominium units, would top the structure starting at the 28th floor and rising to the penthouse on the 68th floor. The views were enhanced by increasing ceiling heights, installing oversize windows, and using the jagged facade to create multiple corners with windows facing different directions. By adding a luxurious health club, fitness room, and other amenities, Trump Tower achieved the highest prices per square foot ever received for condominium units in New York City at the time it was completed. Now that you have a sense of the finished product, let's look at how Trump conceived and executed this fabulous real estate development, and how it paid off for him.

Before Trump Tower was built, the site was owned by the parent company of Bonwit Teller, a fast-fading department store chain. The building was an Art Deco box-like building that had long outlived its usefulness but the location, on 5th Avenue in midtown Manhattan, was one of the most prestigious in the entire city of New York. Although the purchase price for the property was high, Trump believed that the location warranted it and a huge profit would be his if he could maximize the site's potential. Trump believed the ground floor of a new building and the three floors above it could bring very high rents (in excess of $500 per square foot) from major retailers who coveted a 5th Avenue location for a flagship store. He also believed that the high floors with their great views were ideal for the creation of luxury condominium units that would sell for high prices. The middle floors were the problem area that required innovative thinking to obtain maximum benefit from their use and make the investment work. Trump decided to use them as office space knowing full well that it would take creative marketing to get the rents he desired. Thus, Trump's vision of a three-tiered, multi-use condominium building was born. In the late 1970s, a development of this type was very unusual.

One of the lessons for small investors to learn is to find ways, when possible, to put your property to multiple uses, with multiple income streams. If you can create a new use for the property that didn't previously exist, and a new income stream to go along with it, you will have dramatically increased the value of the property when its time to sell or finance. For example, if you have a rental property in the city, you may be able to charge extra for off-street parking, to anyone who lives in the neighborhood. Or you may be able to offer additional services to your tenants, such as Internet service or laundry facilities, for a fee. This strategy also helps to diversify the income from the property so it doesn't come completely from one source (e.g., rents). This makes your income stream from the property less risky, and therefore more valuable.

This multi-use strategy worked brilliantly in Trump Tower, but there were several site-related issues that required resolution before Trump could begin to build. One major problem was the fact that the site consisted of utilizing more than one parcel of land. It included a ground lease on a 25 foot by 100 foot parcel on 57th Street that was owned by Leonard Kandell, an elderly, very savvy real estate developer and investor. Knowing that the ultimate success of the venture hinged on the size of the building he could build on the site, Trump tried to buy Kandell's property but Kandell refused to sell it at any price. Trump's only interest in buying Kandell's parcel was because ownership meant that he would have the right to build a larger building. I enlightened Donald about the zoning laws that permitted one owner to sell and transfer unused building rights (commonly called *air rights*) from his property to the property of an adjacent owner. I told him, "If somehow we can get Kandell's air rights you don't need to own his piece of property." Since Tiffany owned the adjoining property on the corner of 5th Avenue and 57th Street which also had air rights, Trump said, "Tiffany has air rights, too, so I'll buy those." He proceeded to negotiate a deal with Tiffany to buy the air rights over their site.

During his meetings with Walter Hoving, the CEO of Tiffany, Trump learned that Tiffany also had an option to buy Kandell's site for its fair market value. It was a nebulous option at best but Trump felt it would be used as a wedge to get Kandell's cooperation. Trump made sure that the price he paid for Tiffany's air rights also included the option it held on the Kandell site. Then, armed with the Tiffany option, Trump went to Kandell and said, "I'm going to exercise the option to buy your site." Kandell, who was not intimidated in the least, countered with, "You'll have to sue me to exercise the option and I'll fight you every step of the way. The delay would throw your construction timetable into a cocked hat. When you finally win, we'll fight over what amount represents the fair market value of my site." This was shaping up as a classic battle between an unstoppable force meeting an unmovable object. Trump respected Kandell's willingness to fight even though Kandell knew he would ultimately lose his site despite the fact he would receive a high price for it. Trump knew that Kandell had the reputation for being tough but a fair dealer. Sensing the necessity of building a relationship based on mutual respect, Trump called Kandell and asked, "Len, we don't know each other but it's in both our interests to hammer out a deal that we can both live with. What do you want?" Kandell replied, "Donald, although I know you would pay me a lot of money for a deed, I'd like to continue to own my 57th Street site and maybe we can agree on the terms of a long-term ground lease that would include a fair rent which will provide income for my children and grandchildren and give you what you need to build your building."

Relying on his ability to create good business relationships, Trump asked me to join him and Leonard Kandell for lunch at the University Club where Kandell was a member. Trump told Kandell, "Even though I really want to buy your property, I'll let you and George try to work out a great lease that will provide substantial income to your family and give me the flexibility I need." Kandell said, "Thanks, Donald, I appreciate your cooperation." Before Donald left the meeting, he pulled me aside and said, "I've softened Len up, but I really need the new lease ASAP; buying Kandell's property doesn't make sense. Make the lease happen." When I went back to the table, Len Kandell said, "George, before we discuss the terms of a new lease I want you to know I'm going to agree to a lease. If I don't, Donald will buy my site for a lot of money, but I'll have a lot of taxes to pay and I really can't think of a better place to have money invested than 57th Street and 5th Avenue. I leave it up to you to draft a lease that meets Donald's needs but is a fair deal for me." I was shocked by Kandell's simple down-to-earth approach. He was willing to place his trust in me even though he knew I was Trump's lawyer! He said to me, "I know you lawyers are all alike, it will take you months to do a simple lease. At my age I don't have months to spare." I said, "If your lawyer will cooperate I'll have your lease done in two weeks." He said, "I'll bet you can't do it and I'll give you 2 to 1 odds." I accepted the challenge and he put up $2 against my $1. Within two weeks, I prepared and finalized a long-term ground lease with Kandell that gave Trump the air rights he needed and gave Kandell a rental income commensurate with the value of the air rights. One of Kandell's two bucks is still on my wall today. The other I gave to Trump for his cooperation in facilitating the lease negotiations. The creation of the lease was the first step in a long-term friendship between Donald Trump and Leonard Kandell that proved invaluable in future dealings. The lesson for small investors (to reiterate a point made in Chapter 1) is that you should never underestimate the value of good relationships if you are going to be a long-term real estate investor. Both Kandell and Trump were tough negotiators, but they understood this.

Now that he had the air rights he needed to build a building tall enough to justify the high cost of the location, Trump made some very creative and profitable design changes that real estate investors can learn from. He made a concession to New York City, by agreeing to create a pedestrian walkway between 5th Avenue and Madison

Avenue, through the lobby of the commercial portion of Trump Tower. For this concession, the city gave Trump a valuable bonus of additional square footage that he used to increase the number of floors on the most profitable portion of the building, the luxury apartments on the upper floors. But Trump went even farther to create value by flanking the pedestrian walkway with retail stores and showcases, which turned it into a moneymaker. The stores benefited from the increased traffic using the walkway, and the wide walkway with seating areas in the lower level made the public space in the building atrium more attractive to shoppers.

Previously, New York City had passed a statute giving tax benefits to developers who turned underutilized land into residential units. These tax breaks were phased in over 10 years, and Trump was able to pass them along to the buyers of the luxury condominium apartments, which made it much easier to sell the units for the high prices he sought. Small investors should be as savvy as Trump when it comes to knowing about governmental incentives (and restrictions) on developing or renovating property. Sometimes taking advantage of tax breaks and other incentives can be the key to making an investment profitable.

The concept of a mixed-use condominium building such as Trump envisioned was not readily accepted by traditional mortgage lenders, who are conservative by nature. Through his extensive connections, Trump learned that Equitable Life Assurance Company was interested in financing deals in which they also had a piece of the ownership. I negotiated a joint venture agreement between Trump and Equitable whereby Equitable agreed to put up all the money necessary to build Trump Tower. In return, Equitable would eventually receive all of its investment back, plus interest, from the sale of the condominium units. Thereafter, Trump and Equitable would each receive 50 percent of the profits.

But Equitable threw in a clinker that could have soured the deal. Equitable had a policy that a lawyer or law firm that represented

Trump or Equitable in creating the joint venture could not thereafter represent the venture going forward. When I told Trump of this wrinkle he said, "George, if you can't be the lawyer for the venture, I'll kill the Equitable deal." Although I sincerely appreciated his loyalty to me I replied, "Donald, with the Equitable deal you get back your entire investment immediately, all the money you need for construction, and 50% of the profits, it's too good to pass up. I'll still be your lawyer on the deals yet to come." When the joint venture with Equitable was signed I thought I would no longer be involved with Trump Tower. I was wrong.

After I was no longer Trump's lawyer on Trump Tower, Leonard Kandell called me and said, "George, I want you to be my lawyer and handle all my legal matters." I replied, "You'll have to get Donald's okay." He said, "I already did!" I then asked him, "You've got a good lawyer already, why me?" He replied, "When you negotiated and drafted the ground lease, I saw you in action. You're not only a lawyer but you know the real estate business. Whatever you charge, I'll pay." That's how I got Leonard Kandell as a client and even though he died years ago, to this day I still represent his family in real estate matters.

So Trump Tower progressed as the multi-use building as Trump had envisioned. The purpose of the design was to get maximum value out of the three tiers of the structure by creating a condominium with three different ownership levels. The retail stores on the bottom six floors together with the public passageway created a vertical mall, which helped draw people into the building and was a good use of the space because the lower floors have limited views. The commercial office space on floors 4 through 26 offered a prestigious 5th Avenue address along with the high-end services that come with tenancy in a Trump building. This space also houses the Trump Organization headquarters where Donald and I have offices. The Trump-Equitable joint venture maintained ownership of all floors below the 27th floor, and received the high, stable, rents that went with them. The most desirable floors of the building (27 through 68) were devoted to spacious luxury condominiums with incredible views of Central Park and the Manhattan skyline.

Before commencing construction, Trump ran into another snag. Before the building plans were submitted to the Department of Buildings with an application for a building permit, the architects told Trump that the required width of the public walkway through Trump Tower would necessitate the placement of a corner beam straddling the line of the site owned by Kandell. Trump called me as Kandell's new lawyer to get Kandell's consent to an easement permitting the girder to be installed in the requisite location. I spoke to Len Kandell and he asked, "George, does it really diminish the value of my property?" I replied, "No Len, it doesn't, the area Donald needs is 38 feet below street level and only covers a minor piece of your land." Len said, "Tell Donald I'll give my consent gratis." I gave Donald the go ahead. But when the plans for the building were filed with the Department of Building for approval, they came back and insisted that the public walkway be widened even more or it would not be acceptable for the air rights, which would enable Trump to build the building to the height he wanted. I got another call from Donald seeking Kandell's consent to the placement of a beam entirely on Kandell's property. I told him that this was an entirely different request but I would talk to Len Kandell about it. When I told Len Kandell what Donald wanted, he again asked me, "George, does this really diminish the value of my property?" I replied, "Yes, it might, but not much." Len thought a minute and said, "I could probably get Donald to pay me $1 million or $1.5 million for the rights he wants but he's always been fair and square with me, so give it to him for nothing." I told Len that granting Trump the rights he wanted might create a problem with the holder of the mortgage on Kandell's site and if there were a problem I thought Trump should, at least, pay any difference in interest rates between the existing mortgage and any replacement mortgage. Kandell said, "Okay, get Donald to agree to that." When I called Trump, I was curious as to whether or not Kandell was right regarding how much Trump would be willing to pay for the easement he wanted from Kandell. So I called him and teasingly said, "Donald, Len will give you the easement you need but it's going to cost you." Trump asked me, "How much?" I asked him, "Would you pay one million for it?" Without hesitation he said, "Yes." I then said, "Would you pay two million for it?" Donald replied, "That's a high price for just an easement but if that's what Kandell insists upon, I'll pay it." I pushed further and asked, "If I can't get Kandell to do it for less than three million would you still do it?" At that price, Trump exploded and said, "That's outrageous and nothing but a holdup. I'll build Trump Tower without the easement." I countered with, "Donald, this is George, not some novice. The column you want to put on Len's property holds up the corner of the whole building. Don't tell me you don't need it. Would you pay three million if I can't get Kandell to accept less?" After much grumbling, Donald reluctantly agreed to the three million dollar price but said he was furious that Kandell would hold him up for this amount. When I confessed that Kandell had agreed to give it to him for nothing, he was ecstatic. He asked me, "Why would Len do that?" I told him that Kandell felt Donald had treated him fairly when he made a lease that was good for both parties and he considered Donald to be a friend. Trump's ability to build relationships saved him $3 million.

As I mentioned, when Trump Tower was completed in 1983, the concept of a mixed-use building like this was still relatively new. Only the Olympic Tower which had been built in a comparable area, 51st and 5th Avenue, was similar in concept. It was successful but, of course, Trump went one better. He built a building that's unique from an architectural standpoint. By creating an irregular saw-tooth facade, he ended up with rooms with light and views coming from two directions, rather than having rooms with just one window exposure that are found in a typical building with a flat facade. This feature also meant he could plant beautiful trees midway up the structure's facade. While Olympic Tower overlooked St. Patrick's Cathedral, Trump Tower overlooks the greenery of Central Park. Consistent with Trump's flair for showmanship, Trump's signature in this project was the distinctive seven-story cascading waterfall over pink marble inside a spacious tree-lined atrium surrounded by exquisitely matched marble. (Trump reserved the entire Italian quarry just so he could be assured that all the special marble used in Trump Tower would match.) There could be no doubt that Trump had a great vision for this building, but would it be successful as an investment? That depended on finding extremely wealthy buyers to purchase the luxury apartments. As it turned out, there was a backlog of people who wanted something so exciting and exclusive.

A Marketing Masterpiece— Understanding Snob Appeal

When he built Trump Tower, Donald created a market for ultra luxury residential real estate in Manhattan that had not previously existed. He had the foresight to believe that certain kinds of people—celebrities, multimillionaires, chief executives of major corporations, and dignitaries from foreign countries, and others would pay more for the convenience of a luxurious residence within walking distance of their offices and the most prestigious shopping area in central Manhattan. Trump Tower has the ideal and most valuable location in the city, 57th Street and 5th Avenue. Using one of his favorite real estate investing strategies, Trump combined a prime location with innovation.

He took a monumental entrepreneurial risk to execute his vision and to venture into uncharted waters where previously no one had the courage to create a building that targeted this elite, undiscovered market. Trump knew that there are people who willingly pay $250,000 for a Rolls Royce (even though it's still just a car) because of the prestige and the aura associated with the celebrities and the rich people who drive a Rolls. People like to communicate the fact that they have money without specifically broadcasting it. They accomplish this by driving a Rolls Royce, and also by living in Trump Tower. If you own a Rolls Royce, people think you're rich. In the same way, ownership of a unit in Trump Tower equates with being wealthy. People know that owners of apartments in Trump Tower pay up to $20 million for the privilege—a price significantly higher than similarly sized apartments in the neighborhood. They recognize the value of buying ownership of a unit in a Trump building. With such ownership comes the privacy, exclusivity, and the amenities found in a five-star building. As an added bonus, they get what has come to be referred to as the "Trump Touch."

In typical pioneering style, Trump embraced the challenge of creating a product for a market that nobody else dared to enter. Trump believed the market existed, and he was confident that the wealthy would flock to his spectacular building. . . . He even proclaimed, "I will sell residential units at higher prices than anyone else. I will sell units at $1,000 per square foot while owners of similar units elsewhere struggle to get $600 per square foot." Some said that Trump was crazy and his outlandish predictions would never become reality. Trump ended up selling units for $1,000, $1,200, sometimes $1,500 a square foot. The same unit without the Trump name wouldn't sell anywhere near that price; it just wouldn't exhibit the same pizzazz. It wouldn't have snob appeal.

The combination of a desirable location for retail space, offices, and luxury apartments in the same building made Trump Tower a financial success because it maximized the value of each level of the building. Normally, a mix of commercial, office, and residential isn't financially feasible. But by combining a great location with incredible views and stunning architecture, Trump firmly believed he could get higher rents and selling prices per square foot in Trump Tower than anyone else was getting in the city. And he did!

Four Techniques That Dazzle Real Estate Buyers and Tenants

Now let's explore the special elements that added sizzle, glamour, and prestige to Trump Tower. You will also see examples of how small investors can use these same basic techniques to get higher-than-market prices for any kind of property.

Be Distinctive; Add "Sizzle" to Your Property

Trump's trademark is to install an expensive, showy, unique feature in every property, one which will be seen by everyone who enters. An example is the $7 million, 120-foot waterfall at Trump's Westchester golf course. It is seen by everyone who plays there and creates a visual landmark. Golfers stop and admire it, talk about it, and before you know it, even nongolfers vie for the opportunity to play the course just to see it. It's the signature hole that's truly a conversation piece, and it's one of the reasons people will pay $250,000 to become a member at Trump International Golf Course.

Ask yourself: What kind of signature design element could you add to your property that can be seen from the entrance, that would dazzle and impress your buyers or tenants? The core elements in Trump Tower that helped create "sizzle" and sky-high values are:

1. *The Architecture.* Jagged saw-tooth curtain wall on the exterior of the structure that created more views and visual interest than a typical box-type building. Due to this special feature, the view was in two directions from all locations, instead of a one-directional view inherent in ordinary buildings with a flat facade.
2. *Interior Design.* An illuminated seven-story waterfall cascading over finely matched Italian marble in a spacious, thoughtfully designed atrium. Tourists come from all over the world to

photograph this attraction, Trump's signature touch in this development. It was very costly, but everyone who enters the building hears and sees it. It has paid for itself many times over.

3. *Landscaping.* The grove of trees strategically planted along five floors of the facade, at the corner of 56th Street and 5th Avenue.
4. *Location overlooking Central Park*, in the heart of the most important and wealthy business district in America—Midtown Manhattan.

You've seen how Donald Trump does it but you might ask, "How can I, on a much smaller scale, go about adding sizzle and prestige to maximize the value of my property?" The real secret for property of any size is creating something visually striking. It's perceived value. It doesn't have to be expensive, but it has to be *perceived* as valuable. This can be accomplished by a stylish choice of colors, by the type of impressive plantings or desirable amenities so that the potential customer thinks, "This looks like a really nice place to live." It all comes together to create the image of desirability.

What makes something appear desirable? It could be the polished brass hardware or the molding on doors, or the type of wood that the door is made from. It could be window treatments or the immediate availability of maintenance when required. These enhancements are not necessarily expensive. It's the intelligent way of blending creative things together to create the aura of perceived value.

Landscape Design for Visual Impact

Landscaping the exterior should never be overlooked. Even small investors should hire a competent landscape designer. Many are reasonably priced. There is a perceptible harmony to what they do. Designers can create a landscape that reinforces the impression of desirability, without the necessity of costly maintenance. They also have the ability to choose plantings that enhance the topography, the structures, or maximize the size of the site. Instead of arbitrarily putting in three or four bushes, consider planting bushes or shrubs that are carefully chosen to look appropriate in the area and that can be easily maintained and won't become overgrown too quickly. Maybe a small piece of tasteful sculpture or a small fountain could make a problem area a little more attractive while diverting attention away from something negative. Often a piece of sculpture, complemented by careful placement of well-conceived shrubbery, can turn a ho-hum garden area into a showplace. A curved stone or brick walkway bordered with attractive plantings is another desirable feature for any property.

Trump takes landscaping very seriously. At Trump International Golf Course in Florida, Donald had 2,000 trees transplanted—and these weren't little trees, they were big—which made a spectacular impact and beautified the property. This was in addition to hundreds of bushes and shrubs planted on or around the golf course. In all, over 1.3 million cubic yards of earth was utilized to develop the facility. (That's the equivalent of approximately 144,500 cement trucks full of dirt.) Trump raised the height of the 18th tee to 80 feet, making it the highest elevation in Palm Beach County. He transformed the site into a spectacular golf course. This is how Trump does it. He makes all of his projects exclusive and different from what others choose to create.

You don't have to plant 2,000 trees on your property, but you can find a way to make your landscaping distinctive. Landscape designers come in all sizes. Get someone who is up and coming, and who really wants to make it big. If you hire people who are good, you use them on future properties. To induce them you might say, "Look, this is the first four-unit building I have purchased, but I intend to buy six more and I would like to use your expertise for all of them." If you can get your landscape designer excited about future work he or she will be motivated to do an exceptional job.

Once a potential occupant perceives the exterior of your building to be a nice place to live or work, the inside must visually seal the sale.

GIVE YOUR CUSTOMERS THE ULTIMATE IN
PERCEIVED QUALITY

The key principle here is "spend money where it can be seen." For example, Trump pays more for chairs in lobbies and atriums than those in interior rooms. He would, for example, easily pay $15,000 for a piece of furniture in the clubhouse of Mar-a-Lago, his Palm Beach country club, because it's in a strategic location where people are going to see it. Trump tries to use whatever works to attract a person looking for luxury, but his credo is "spend money where it can be seen."

Small real estate investors need to ask themselves, "What can I do with this property that no one else is doing—to make it distinctive?" The answer is to try to get away from the commonplace and give tenants and buyers more than they might expect. You can often do this by adding small, but impressive upgrades to your property. This requires vision and creativity, and an intuitive sense for what will impress people. If you don't have this aesthetic sense yourself, you can hire an architect or designer who does, provided he or she knows how to work within your budget. Trump found a way to sell apartments at unheard of prices: $1,000 or more per square foot when everyone else was struggling to get $600. Ask yourself, what design elements could I build or renovate into my property that would make it more desirable than any competing property of its type in its neighborhood? With some concentrated effort, you can find the answer.

Be willing to overpay on a few critical details of your building or renovation project; the aesthetics must be dramatic and draw people in and impress them. You can use large entry rooms to make a statement. Spaciousness is always distinctive. For example, the upper level residential units in Trump Tower have much higher than typical ceilings, which make the units appear more spacious, which in turn gives the units a greater perceived value. Try to incorporate higher ceilings in your plans if your budget permits.

The flip side of spending money on entrances and key public spaces is, "Don't spend money where people aren't going to see it." Don't put double beams where single beams are adequate. As far as cost, Trump will overpay to get the right look where it will be seen. You won't gain anything by overspending in an unseen area. If, for example, there are two different methods of construction, both of which are perfectly acceptable from a technical point of view, and it's not in a visible area, why choose the more expensive method?

Kitchens and Bathrooms Seal the Deal

If you're building or renovating residences, every successful builder knows that the most important rooms in houses or apartments as far as occupants are concerned are kitchens and bathrooms. Extra dollars spent in those rooms will reap big rewards either in sales price or rentals. If you skimp on costs in your kitchen and bathroom, you'll have a problem attracting the upscale buyer. These two rooms are what sell houses more than anything else. Not bedrooms. The first thing the buyer of the house looks for are functional and appealing kitchens and bathrooms. There's an old saying in real estate sales that goes like this: When a man and woman are thinking of buying a house, the first thing the woman considers is the kitchen and bathrooms: the man's first consideration is how much the mortgage payments will be.

For kitchens, consider installing countertops of granite, stilestone, or a solid surface material such as Corian or Avonite. It's expensive but eye-catching and creates the perceived value you strive to achieve. Size, color, and placement of appliances are great selling points. A Sub-Zero built-in refrigerator instead of a Kenmore can influence the buyer's decision. Don't skimp when it comes to kitchen cabinets and the pantry. You want a potential buyer to think, "I can see myself living and working in this kitchen. It's beautiful, and it's got everything I want."

When it comes to bathrooms, try to make them as spacious as circumstances allow. Put extra dollars in countertops, vanities, and lighting fixtures. The bathtub should be a Jacuzzi, if feasible. Storage space and soothing color combinations are necessities.

Another winning feature is closets with built-ins such as shoe racks and adjustable shelving. Always ask yourself, "Where can I spend my renovation or building money to make the greatest visual impact?" Put your money on the answer.

Lawrence Welk and the $50/Yard Carpeting

Here's a great example of a real estate investor who added "the Trump Touch" to his property, with great results. I have a friend in Los Angeles who in the late 1970s was married to the resident manager for one of Lawrence Welk's buildings. (In case you're too young to remember, Lawrence Welk had his own hit television show which ran for 17 years during the 1970s and 1980s.) With the huge profits from the show, Welk invested heavily in southern California real estate, including Champagne Towers, a very exclusive high-rise apartment building that overlooked the Santa Monica Pier and the Pacific Ocean. This friend purchased a 20-unit fixer-upper in a rough part of south central Los Angeles. Meanwhile, his wife Peggy, the manager of Champagne Towers, was responsible for replacing the carpet every time a tenant moved out of Champagne Towers, with new carpet of the tenant's choice. The carpeting being replaced was very expensive, top-of-the-line stuff that cost $50/yard and in many cases was hardly used. So my friend bought it from his wife (at the market price for used carpet of $1/square yard) and began installing it in the 20-unit building he owned. Now imagine this thick, plush "Berber-like" carpeting being installed in ghetto-like apartments in a very rough neighborhood. The buzz among the building's residents was unbelievable. The resident manager had to create a waiting list for people in the neighborhood who had heard about the carpeting and wanted to live there. My friend was able to receive higher rents, and the building seldom had vacancies, all because of this fancy carpet. It had the same effect as if the whole building had been renovated, but for a fraction of the cost. The moral is, look for cost-effective ways to impress your buyers and tenants. You may pay a little more than your competition, but if it enables you to charge more rent or get a higher selling price, it's worth it.

A Word of Caution: Never lose your focus on the bottom line of your investment. It is possible to lose control and spend too much on upgrades, even though the reality is that most real estate investors probably don't spend enough. It is important to create a spreadsheet listing all anticipated costs associated with your property's acquisition, possible holding periods, construction, and marketing. After considering all the expense items, give careful thought to the anticipated income. Strike a balance between unbridled enthusiasm and realism in your financial projections. If the result meets your expectations, go for it!

UNDERSTAND YOUR BUYERS' AND TENANTS' LIFESTYLE

Before proceeding with any real estate venture, you have to determine what's appropriate for your particular project. You must familiarize yourself with the surrounding neighborhood and the life style and income of the people you are planning to sell or rent to. To accomplish this, you have to do your homework, which includes doing research and learning as much as you can about your potential customers. Canvass other projects in the area; speak to brokers whose livelihood comes from the sales or leasing of units. If you portray yourself as a potential buyer or renter, brokers will deluge you with loads of information that you can distill to reality. Find out what amenities are being offered by other developers building properties similar to yours.

When he designed Trump Tower with luxury condominiums, Trump recognized the fact that there are well-paid major executives in all the big corporations, and that many movie stars and celebrities would want a prestigious building in a prime location—and would pay a premium price. Many owners travel extensively and use their units as a home away from home while they're in New York City. Executives of big corporations, especially foreign executives from Europe or Asia, want a place in a convenient location where they can entertain guests in plush surroundings and be comfortable. Trump Tower's location, at 56th Street and 5th Avenue, which is in walking distance of all the major buildings in Manhattan, was ideal. They could buy a residential unit in the corporate name and use it as their headquarters while they're in the city.

Trump Tower offers residents numerous amenities such as a beautiful spa and fitness facility, concierge service, separate attended elevators, 24-hour doorman, whose duties include hailing taxicabs, accepting packages, and calling you when your limousine arrives. Small investors can do the same thing on a different scale by offering buyers or tenants special amenities that will impress them and sell them on your site.

Use Feng Shui to Boost Property Values

Here's a case in point which demonstrates the importance of understanding your customers' lifestyle. This example is Trump International Tower on Columbus Circle in New York City. During the planning stages, Trump knew Asians were a likely source of potential buyers, and that the building he was constructing should cater to their desires. So he had feng shui experts advise him on the design of the building. *Feng shui* is an ancient Chinese philosophy involving the relationship of individuals with their surroundings. It's a standard of practice for creating the ideal environment in which to live and

Trump International Hotel and Tower

work. Essentially, it's a philosophy that distinguishes good signs from bad signs, and teaches methods of design that are in harmony with nature and the surrounding area. The Asian populace embraces it. They will not buy into any building if the principles of feng shui have been violated. The feng shui experts' analysis of this site told Trump that certain aspects of the building did not comply with the laws of feng shui. Relying on their opinion, Trump redesigned the location of the building entrance so that it would be in harmony with the surrounding area. Trump even had the building blessed in a special ceremony conducted by feng shui experts and, of course, he made sure there was a lot of publicity about it which found its way into the Asian media. The fact that Trump showed his concern for Asian culture, and spent a lot of money and time to do it, attracted Asian people to the building. The owner's sensitivity to their special requirements was a major inducement.

KNOW WHAT YOUR CUSTOMERS WILL PAY EXTRA FOR AND WHAT THEY WON'T

The probability of attention-getting "extras" paying off strictly depends on the location and type of real estate project you are investing in. For example, if you're refurbishing a four-unit residential building, you should canvass other comparable buildings in the area to find out what they offer as "building standard" and what typical rental rates have been achieved. For this type of project, the items to be considered in building standard would be carpeting; painting; kitchen appliances and cabinets; air conditioning units; television access by means of an antenna, cable, or satellite; and lighting fixtures to name a few. Unless you're certain that your tenants would pay a higher rental for a building standard that includes items that would normally be "extras," I suggest that you offer the tenant optional upgrades that you would be willing to supply for a higher rental rate. For example, the building standard refrigerator could have a 17.5 cu. ft. capacity but an option could be one of higher capacity. Standard kitchen countertops could consist of Formica or similar laminates. Options could include granite, ceramic tile, or solid surface materials such as Corian or Stilestone, the extra cost of which is included in the rent.

In any real estate deal, it's important for you to identify your target audience and focus your attention on accommodating it. If your target is middle-class families and you elect to provide amenities typically found in developments catering to those with higher incomes, you won't recoup the extra expense. However it is a fact that most people, no matter their income level, will pay a little more for luxury. Although you may be targeting middle-income buyers, you should identify the cost-effective upgrades that will dazzle them and make them willing to pay a little more than they otherwise would. People who can afford luxury will recognize more extravagant extra touches such as heightened security, 24-hour doormen, and closed-circuit cameras or gated and manned entry areas. These are things they can appreciate as having added value. Unfortunately, the lines between low-income families, middle-income families, and high-income families are blurry at best and difficult to pin down. After you've obtained all the knowledge of your likely buyers or tenants as you can, then go after that target. Having said that, be willing to quickly revise your ideas about what your customers want, if you learn new facts that warrant such a change. Success in any real estate venture has a direct relationship to appropriate timing and the changes in circumstances that occur in any timeframe. Be aware of everything that's happening in the local economic and real estate climate that could affect your decision making. Smart real estate investors, just like entrepreneurs in general, have to stay flexible.

6

Raising Money

Tactics for Attracting Lenders and Investors

Key Points

- Make lenders want to do business with you.
- Borrow as much as you can for as long as you can.
- Borrow from a lender with whom you already have a relationship.
- Don't sweat the details.
- How to get investors.
- Mortgage alternatives for small investors.

R AISING MONEY, WHETHER it's derived from investors, family, friends, or borrowed from commercial lenders, is one of the most crucial elements in any real estate transaction. The use of borrowed money to buy real estate serves several purposes: It gives you more leverage, which enables you to purchase much more, often 20 or 30 times more than what could otherwise be bought for cash; it reduces your equity exposure; and the interest payments on the loan provide a significant tax deduction.

When Trump invests in a real estate project, he typically puts up less of his own money than you might think. For example, he will often erect a building to either rent out the available space or sell the residential units in it. Typically, his investors in the project will put up 85 percent while Trump puts up 15 percent. Then he and his partners get a fixed rate of return on their cash investments. However, the return accrues and is not paid until there are cash proceeds to distribute. When units are sold, Trump uses the excess funds over and above the mortgage to be applied to the accrued interest. When the accrued interest has been paid, available funds are used to repay the cash investment of the partners. When all partners get back all their money plus the accrued interest, additional proceeds are divided among the partners. But the split of the excess funds is no longer 85 percent for the partners and 15 percent for Trump. Now the split of the profits could be 50–50, 40–60, or 25–75, depending on certain variables inherent in the transaction. It depends on the interest rate paid to the outside partners. The higher the rate of interest the outside partners get, the lower the percentage they get. The lower the rate of interest paid to the outside partners, the higher the percentage they get. Keep in mind the huge size of Trump projects, and that relatively speaking, 15 percent is a big number. If we're talking about building a $300 million building, then 15 percent represents $45 million.

Trump often has some group or large company participating as a partner. It may be a huge corporation such as General Motors (GM) or General Electric (GE). With partners such as these, Trump can get a very favorable large loan well below the prime rate and often without the need for a mortgage and payment of the recording taxes involved. Without these types of partners, Trump could never get that kind of a loan. When GM borrows from a bank, they get a low rate based on their credit, so Trump likes to work with these kinds of partners.

Working with monied outside investors enables him to participate in many transactions without a monster exposure of dollars in a particular development. The Trump Organization furnishes the time, the effort, the expertise, the staff, and the management for the entire project. The sole function of the outside investors is financial.

Small investors can and should use a similar approach in financing their real estate investments. This chapter describes key principles for raising money from banks and investors, such as establishing lender relationships, knowing how much to borrow, and knowing methods of attracting investors. These are all instrumental to successfully investing in real estate, regardless of the scale of your project. By following Trump's principles for real estate financing set forth in this chapter, you can also avoid the costliest mistake many investors make—using short-term money for long-term projects.

INVESTING CASE STUDY

THE GM BUILDING

The GM Building in New York City is massive. Built by General Motors as its headquarters, it's a two-million square-foot 50-story structure that fronts on 5th Avenue and Madison Avenue at the southeast corner of Central Park in Manhattan. It is one of the few buildings in the world that takes up an entire square block bounded by two major avenues. It is regarded as the premier office building in New York City.

When the property came up for sale in 1998 by a real estate investment trust, Trump felt he had to have it. However, one of the major drawbacks was a long-term lease of 400,000 square feet with a major law firm at a very low rent with many options for additional space as well as renewal terms. So, in effect, 20 percent of the building was frozen from future growth. That lease, together with other long-term leases at below market rents, were key negative factors. On the positive side, the building was prestigious, had a great location, and the tenancy consisted of companies or individuals that were giants in the business world making the building extremely attractive to major lenders who wanted the security of a stable rental stream.

The sales price of the GM Building was $800 million—all cash. The challenge Trump faced was obtaining a huge mortgage loan at a low interest rate, raising money for the balance of the purchase price, and raising sufficient working capital since the existing cash flow was anemic. The solution was finding a partner with deep pockets who could be induced to participate in a massive undertaking.

Quite by accident, Trump met Steve Hilberg who was the CEO of the Conseco insurance group, a public company loaded with money. They became friends and Trump proposed a plan in which he and Conseco would become partners, buy the GM Building, and make a profit of $300 million within one year by turning the building into an office condominium. Since major corporations had big blocks of space, Trump believed that they would rather buy the space they occupied than face a major increase in rent when their respective leases expired. Hilberg liked the concept especially since Donald Trump, who was a superstar in New York City real estate, proposed it.

GM Building

They formed a joint venture in which Conseco agreed to put up the bulk of the money over a new mortgage loan that Trump was able to obtain.

Trump made a deal with Lehman Brothers that for a substantial fee they would commit to fund $700 million at a low interest rate acceptable to Trump. This amount—$700 million—was almost 90 percent of the purchase price—a very high loan to value ratio. Since the loan was top heavy, Lehman required some guarantee to induce institutional investors to participate. Trump persuaded Conseco to give the lenders the guarantee they wanted, to cover what the lenders perceived to be excess loan proceeds. In order to achieve a low interest rate, Lehman had to syndicate the loan (i.e., split the loan into several pieces, each of which would have a different degree of risk and a different interest rate, and would be sold to a different investor). The first mortgage loan of $500 million was layered in $100 million increments. The lender with the bottom layer would have the highest priority of payment, but would receive the lowest rate of interest. The lender with the top layer would have the lowest priority of payment but the highest rate of interest.

For the remaining $200 million of proceeds, a secondary loan was created that was subordinate to the primary loan of $500 million. In a manner similar to the primary loan, the secondary was also layered to cater to investors who had different appetites for risk and reward. The secondary financing was coupled with the Conseco guarantee so that it would carry a lower interest rate than one without a guarantee. Conseco and Trump funded any additional funds required to purchase the building as required under the joint venture agreement. When and if additional monies were required for improvements or other business purposes both Conseco and Trump would fund their proportionate shares by means of interest bearing loans.

As I mentioned, the building was purchased with the intention of transforming it into a commercial condominium and selling the units to the existing tenants (GM, Estee Lauder, etc.) plus other Fortune 500 companies desiring offices in what was considered to be one of the most prestigious office buildings in New York City. Although office building condominiums were popular and successful outside of New York City, that trend had not worked in New York. Developers who tried it were unsuccessful and usually abandoned the concept. Undaunted by this track record, Trump filed a condominium plan for the building and the state attorney general approved it.

Recognizing the possibility that the condominium concept might fail, Trump told me that my number one priority was to position the building to prospective tenants in such a way that it could command rents of $100 per square foot—an amount never before achieved by office buildings in New York City. He said that he would make the necessary improvements to attract tenants willing to pay top dollar for luxury. I said, "Donald, if you do that and we give the building the 'Trump touch,' I'll get you the rent you're looking for." True to his word, Trump started his extensive and expensive renovation plan. I obtained possession of all the commercial space in the unsightly, open, lower-level commercial area known in the trade as "the pit." Trump transformed it into a new, tree-lined, aesthetically pleasing plaza area above street level. This created a direct, impressive 5th Avenue entrance that the building never had.

The main entrance lobby was still being used as display space for GM cars. Donald said, "George, I hate those cars. Figure out a way to get rid of them, so I can make the lobby a showplace." When I learned that GM was planning on selling its lease on the ground floor to CBS but needed the landlord's cooperation to make it happen, I used that as a wedge to get the cars out of the lobby and leased a substantial amount of space to CBS. Once the cars were gone, Trump rebuilt the lobby with magnificent marble floors with brass inserts and new lighting which enhanced the beauty. A striking 40-foot security/reception desk was installed with an equally striking ancillary concierge desk flanking it. All the building systems, such as electric, plumbing, and fire safety, were upgraded to be the latest technology available. All elevator cabs were refurbished and new mechanical components installed. Agreements were reached with all major telephone and data transmission services to provide tenants with access to the latest technology. Originally there were two entrances on Madison Avenue, one on each side of a Barbie Doll store run by FAO Schwarz. We made a deal with FAO to give up the Barbie store so that we could create one integrated building entrance flanked by two new stores. In return, FAO would get 50 percent of rent received in excess of the reduction it received when FAO gave up the Barbie store.

Everything I have mentioned didn't happen overnight but over a period of three years. During that period, some unusual things happened. I hired two major real estate brokerage firms to act as co-leasing agents for the building. When we bought the building, the prior owner had offered to extend the lease of an affiliate of U.S. Steel Corporation at a rental of $50 a square foot. The brokers thought that was a good rental for 9th floor space and represented a 25 percent increase. I disagreed and told them I would consider $90 a square foot. The brokers ultimately got the tenant to agree to $65 a square foot and set up a meeting with me to convince me to take it because that was the maximum rent the tenant would agree to pay and was a 62.5 percent increase. I refused telling them I anticipated getting rent of $100 a square foot or more after Trump did his magic. One of the brokers said, "George, you'll never see more than $65 a square foot for space in the GM Building!" Shortly after that meeting I fired that broker. If he didn't share the vision, how could he sell it to others?

When the building was bought we assumed there would be very little activity since it had virtually no vacancy and very few leases were close to expiration. That assumption proved to be wrong. A tenant on the 50th floor paying a low rental wanted out of their lease that had about two years to go. They paid me a healthy amount of money to assume their obligation. That space was subsequently rented for $100 a square foot, proving our assessment of the rent potential was correct. Other tenants of the building also desired to vacate early and, each time, I agreed to assume their obligations since we were always well paid to do so. Within a period of three years, we received over $14 million in payments from tenants for the right to vacate before their leases expired. In each instance, we were able to rent the space to a new tenant at rentals ranging from $85 a square foot to $115 a square foot. Based on these results and the inability to get the requisite number of buyers necessary to declare the office condominium plan effective, I suggested to Trump and Conseco that they switch plans and reconsider the building as a long-term investment until its full potential could be achieved. Conseco agreed and based on its recognition of Trump's stellar performance agreed to lower the interest rate on their investment. In preparation for a refinancing, I commissioned the independent appraiser who did the original appraisal when the building was purchased to do a revised appraisal based on the new rents we were getting, and the new "Trump Touch" the building now had. He reappraised the building at $1.2 billion—an increase of $400 million in just four years! In 2003, Conseco was suffering financially and they insisted that the building be sold at auction. The sale price was $1.4 billion dollars creating a profit of about $500 million dollars that was shared by Trump and Conseco.

Make Lenders Want to Do Business with You

It's highly unlikely that any of my readers need to borrow $700 million to buy the equivalent of the GM Building, but every real estate investor needs financing of some kind. How do you go about finding a lender willing to loan you money? If you have a good credit record, banks will be willing to loan you money. However, most new investors try to borrow money only when they need it. That's a mistake. It's when you don't need money that banks are most inclined to give you a loan! When your financial position is strong, their risk is lower and you are an attractive borrower. When you really need a loan, the lender will ask you why you need it and then reach their own assessment of the reason you give. Don't let banks do this. Don't let banks make business decisions for you; their business is lending money not making real estate deals. They are conservative by nature. Real estate investors are risk takers by choice.

Here's a simple method of establishing credit that I have used to great advantage. Go to a bank and ask to borrow $10,000. When they ask you the reason for the loan tell them you want to be able to make an investment when an opportunity presents itself. When the bank asks for your financial statement (which you should have prepared before your meeting and have with you) give it to them. To the extent you have some asset that can be reduced to cash such as stocks, bonds, or surrender value of insurance policies, offer it as security for the loan even though the value far exceeds the amount of the loan you asked for. Remember, you're borrowing simply for the purpose of establishing credit. One essential ingredient is that you always have the right to prepay the loan at any time without penalty. Essentially, what you want to do is, borrow $10,000, pay it back, then borrow $25,000, pay it back, then borrow $50,000, pay it back, and so on. You want to establish a perfect payment record. If you put the borrowed money in another account that earns interest, all you really lose is the difference in the interest rate you pay the bank and the rate you earn on the investment of the loan proceeds. Along the way, ask the bank to return or reduce your security based on your excellent credit record. If they balk, tell them you're contemplating taking your account to another bank that's more flexible. If your loan officer says no, talk to his superior who will probably be more receptive to your request. If you keep pushing the bank to increase the loan amounts, make all payments in a timely fashion and if your latest financial statement is sound, when you really need a sizable loan your bank will be there without questioning the wisdom of your investment plans. Of course, this violates normal bank policy. But it happens all the time with a bank's good customers with whom they have an established relationship. Your goal should be to get banks to trust your judgment and trustworthiness based on your track record, so you can get money when you need it without the typical inquisition.

My reasoning may sound far-fetched but you have to keep in mind that banks don't like to lose business from a good customer. If you have a good track record with a bank, and they refuse to make you an unsecured loan, you can tell them, "I've been banking here for years. My credit history is impeccable and I've enjoyed the relationship. But if you can't see your way clear to increase my credit line, I'll have to find another bank who will appreciate me as a customer." Banks will lean over backward not to lose good borrowers with a proven track record.

Lessons on Raising Money: First-Time Borrowers

The application of pressure from the right people in the right places can make the difference for a borrower. If, for example, you have a friend who knows the bank officer you're dealing with, that could be the item that tips the scale in your favor, as it was for me. You want someone with a great banking relationship to say, "I have known this guy for years, he's great, and I know that he will live up to all his financial obligations." Good recommendations go a long way in loan or investment decision making.

Also, a real estate broker with whom you're doing business or intending to do business could be very helpful in obtaining financing. He or she is likely to have developed contacts with mortgage lenders who have made or may be interested in making loans of the type you are seeking. Agree to pay them a commission if they are successful in obtaining a loan you find acceptable. Depending on the size and reputation of the broker, there may be several different lenders willing to make the investment and you can pick and choose. Any help you can get from any source is better than going in cold. Spend time establishing a network of people who can be useful in turning a "no" into a "yes."

By George . . . Building a Credit History with Banks and Investors

Early in my career when I first decided to invest in real estate, I was given an outstanding opportunity to invest in mortgages. Recognizing my inexperience in raising money, Alex DiLorenzo Jr., one of the two partners in the real estate firm I worked for, said to me, "George, I'm going to let you place a first mortgage on a good piece of property. It will be $35,000 for one year with interest paid monthly at an annual rate of 16 percent. Even though the property is worth $75,000, Sol and I (two multimillionaires) will personally guarantee all payments. Now you go out and raise the $35,000. I'm going to show you how difficult it is to get money from people even for a good deal."

I thought this was a piece of cake since I had already lined up a number of personal friends and relatives that told me they had money to invest. A typical first response was, "George, I have full faith in you and whatever you think is a good investment. I'm behind you 100 percent. Just tell me how much you need and when. You can count on me." However, when the time came to write out the checks, the same people got cold feet and came up with various lame excuses to explain their refusal to participate. I had already assured Alex that I would make the mortgage loan and I didn't want to lose face. I got $5,000 from my mother-in-law but that was all I could get from any outside investors.

(Continued)

So I went to the bank in the Chrysler Building where my office was located and said, "I want to borrow $30,000 to make a mortgage loan. Here's my background, I've been a lawyer 10 years, I make a good salary, I own my own house, and here's a list of my assets. As you can see, I'm good for the money." The bank officer said, "You're planning to invest in mortgages. I don't like that kind of investment."

I replied, "I didn't ask you for investment advice, I asked you to determine if I'm worth $30,000 on the hoof!"

He said, "No." I couldn't believe the turndown. It was the first time I had ever applied for a personal loan and I thought I would be received with open arms.

My brother-in-law Martin Beck had a good friend who was a loan officer in a small bank and he suggested that I see this loan officer for the $30,000 loan I needed. The banker said, "Okay, give me the mortgage as collateral and I'll lend you the $30,000." I am certain that he made the loan only out of friendship with Marty, not based on my financial standing.

So I put up the money for the $35,000 mortgage. Like clockwork I made monthly payments to my mother-in-law for her share of the investment. Then, to my delight, she started telling all her friends and others who would listen that she invested money with me at 16 percent interest and was receiving a check by the 5th of each month. They said, "How can we get into a deal like that?" She told them to call me and see if I would let them in on my next deal. I also told all my potential investors who backed out what a mistake they had made and their money could have been earning 16 percent a year instead of the meager 3 percent a year their bank was paying.

Because of my newfound fame, the next time around I had no problem getting investors—but I cut down the amount I was willing to let each person invest in the deal. There's nothing like telling a willing investor, "I can't let you in for $ 30,000 but I can give you a $20,000 piece. I'm oversubscribed as it is but for you I'll make room." Now that they believed I had many other investors clamoring to let me invest their money in my deals, it was no longer a problem to get whatever money I needed from investors. The investors I restricted told their friends and relatives about the wonderful investment opportunity they got into even though others were refused.

Because I only made short-term loans on property I was familiar with, and repayment was guaranteed by my wealthy employers, I had no bad loans. Because my loans were at an annual interest rate of 16 percent or more and I only paid my investors a healthy 10 percent, I was creating a lot of income from the spread. It became clear to me that if I could borrow the money from a bank I wouldn't have to pay 10 percent a year on borrowed funds but only the lesser rate the bank would charge. So, what I did was to pay off the original $30,000 that I had borrowed from the bank, long before it was due. Although I didn't need any money until I was ready to place another mortgage, I then asked the bank to loan me $50,000. They asked, "What are you going to do with the money?" "I'm going to invest it." was my reply. They asked, "What are you going to invest in?" I told them that I didn't know right now but I wanted to be able to move quickly when something came up. In the interim, I would leave the money I borrowed in my bank account with them until I needed it. They loved the idea and since I had already repaid the $30,000 and my financial statement now reflected increased income, they approved the $50,000 loan. I eventually paid off the $50,000 ahead of schedule. Shortly thereafter, I asked for a loan of $100,000 but they would only approve it for $80,000. I accepted the reduction and again paid it off ahead of time. Over the years, I have developed a $500,000 unsecured line of credit with a series of banks just by their review of my credit history and financial statement that showed my ownership of many high-interest paying mortgages. If one loan officer said his authority was limited, I said, "Tell me whose approval is needed." I then went up the ladder of authority and established a relationship with the higher ups. I also used existing loan officers as a credit reference for new banks with which I was creating a new relationship.

(Continued)

Small real estate investors can take the same approach by borrowing small amounts, investing it wisely, paying the loan back promptly, or ahead of time, and then subsequently asking to borrow more. This approach requires that you start small, but it can lead to a very large credit line, and is the foundation of any real estate investor's ability to get financing, whether you are dealing with banks or private investors. It is extremely important to never forget that the key to borrowing money or attracting investors is establishment of trustworthiness. If you promise something, especially money, deliver it when and how you said you would. A happy lender or investor is your best salesman for attracting new ones.

BORROW AS MUCH AS YOU CAN FOR AS LONG AS YOU CAN

The theory behind this is simple. If the loan market goes well (i.e., interest rates go down), and you have a right of prepayment without a major penalty, you can effectively refinance at a lower interest rate and save money. If the market goes sour (interest rates go up), you don't have to worry about refinancing because the rate you're paying is probably lower than the then higher prevailing market rate of interest. But that's only part of the story. Remember that the key to a successful investment strategy is to have extra money on hand that you have no immediate use for! If you keep yourself liquid then you can act when an opportunity presents itself, which often occurs when money is tight and there are few buyers with significant cash in the market. The fact that you have available cash enables you to snap up the bargains that are available. Two other factors to consider are that loan proceeds are not treated as taxable income and interest paid on loans for business purposes is deductible from taxable income. The proper leveraging of borrowed money can save you many dollars that otherwise would go to the government.

Borrowing as much as you can for as long as you can doesn't necessarily mean that you should seek a loan in excess of the value of the asset you're pledging. But don't think that's a terrible idea. If you mortgage a property for more than your investment in it, you have a built-in profit even if you can't pay the mortgage at maturity. Failure to pay a loan at maturity is the basis for foreclosure and potential loss of property and any equity that you may have in it. However, if the value of any real estate has dropped precipitously since you financed it, a loss by foreclosure may be better than continually adding money to protect your investment when the possibility of recovery is very slim. The less money you have in it at that time, the better it is for you.

Why Shopping for a Home Mortgage Is Important

Did you know that the most expensive thing you'll likely ever buy is not your home—it's the cost of *financing* required to purchase that home. Over the long run, you'll pay more in interest than you will pay for your house. Many home buyers fail to take into consideration the aggregate interest cost of the mortgage placed on their home. For example, suppose you buy a home for $165,000 and borrow $150,000 at 7 percent for 30 years. That mortgage, if amortized over the entire 30-year term, will cost you $359, 640—which is more than twice the amount you borrowed, and more than double the price of the home. Now in a different scenario, if you bought the same home and borrowed the same amount of $150,000, but instead took out a cheaper mortgage at 6 percent for 30 years—a seemingly meager 1 percent differential from the 7 percent mortgage—look at the aggregate savings. The cheaper 6 percent mortgage, if amortized over the same 30-year term, will cost you $324,000, a savings of $35,640. Since home ownership is a long-term investment (in contrast with many business investments), financing conservatively, at fixed rates, without excessively high payments, is without a doubt the best approach to take. It is important for your peace of mind to know your home is never in jeopardy.

Fixed-Rate versus Variable-Rate Mortgages

With a fixed-rate mortgage, you know what your payments will be from the day you placed the mortgage to the day it matures. You don't know what your payments will be with an adjustable rate mortgage (ARM). Banks often entice borrowers with a low interest rate on an ARM to start with but you're really subject to economic changes over which you have absolutely no control. If you think a variable-rate mortgage is for you, try to negotiate for a "cap" (i.e., the maximum interest rate you will be required to pay). If, for example, you take out a 5.5 percent loan with a cap of 8 percent, the interest rate on the loan can never go above 8 percent. Even if this protection costs something, it's usually worth it. If, in exchange for giving you a cap the bank insists on your agreeing to a "floor" (i.e., the lowest rate of interest the bank will receive), the added protection is still desirable if the loan has a duration of more than two or three years. The only time a variable-rate mortgage may be better than a fixed-rate loan is in the very short term, say three years or less, if it allows you to take advantage of a low initial "teaser" rate, which usually takes about three years to be adjusted upward. If you intend to own your house for the long term (i.e., more than three years) then a fixed-rate loan will let you sleep at night.

As I write this book, I am certain there are many home owners succumbing to the lure of a long-term variable-rate mortgage with a very low rate of interest for the first year. We in the United States are spoiled because our rate of inflation has been low for so many years. The rest of the world hasn't been so lucky. Some countries have annual inflation exceeding 100 percent. Don't think that could never happen here.

Lessons on Leverage and Time

How can you minimize risk when financing real estate? Remember another cardinal rule: *Don't make long-term investments with short-term money.* Therefore, when you get a mortgage, negotiate for the right to extend the term even if there's a payment attached for the privilege of doing so. Say you have investors and you promise to pay them off in whole or in part in three years. Insert a safety valve provision in the loan documents: If it's not paid back in three years, you have the right to extend it for a period of up to six years at a higher rate of interest. This way you have the luxury of an additional three years if you need it.

Bridge loans are another way to protect against the unavailability of money at a future date. It's possible to get one type of financing (a *bridge loan*) to cover a certain activity (e.g., construction or renovation of a property). At the same time, you get a commitment for another loan (the *takeout loan*) that is contingent upon the completion of that activity and meeting certain criteria that the takeout lender sets forth in the commitment to determine the amount of money that will be paid out when the takeout loan is funded. The fees that the takeout lender will require to issue the loan are highly negotiable depending on the foreseeable degree of risk. If, after the renovation or construction is completed, the property will be sold, there is a distinct possibility that the amount to be funded by the takeout lender will be minimal but the fee for the commitment is based on the possibility that the entire amount of the takeout loan will be funded. That's how takeout lenders make a lot of money, especially if there's a long time before completion of the construction or the renovation.

However the existence of a commitment for a takeout loan may be a prerequisite of the bridge lender. It is possible for the bridge lender and the takeout lender to be the same party, although the terms of the bridge loan and the takeout loan could be substantially different. But most lenders pursue a single role rather than a dual one.

Borrow from a Lender with Whom You Already Have a Relationship

You need to develop a working relationship with one or more commercial lenders if you have a sincere desire to be in the *business* of real estate investing. It is equally important to develop similar relationships with potential investors. Remember if you do a good job on your first project, see that the word gets out and it will be a lot easier to get investors on your next project because nothing succeeds like success. Don't be timid when it comes to boasting about your accomplishments; use photographs and any favorable publicity your property has received.

Don't Sweat the Details

Keep in mind that banks, or for that matter any type of commercial lender, have their own lending philosophies and ways of doing business and preparing documents. Don't expect to win much in negotiating the details of your loan agreement. With the exception of interest rates, terms of payment, rights of prepayment, and maturity dates, you'll have to accept the language contained in the lender's loan documents. You can rely on the fact that banks are extremely reluctant to call in a loan that is being paid in a timely fashion even when many technical defaults exist. If more than one lender participates in making your loan, the chance of their pursuit of a technical default is even more remote. Bankers hate to deal with problem loans—especially when timely payments are being made.

How to Get Investors

Trump has loads of available cash, but he still seeks investors so he can invest in several large projects concurrently. Bringing in equity investors effectively reduces Trump's risk on any given project, while the money provided by equity partners makes it easier to get better financing. The more capital invested by a borrower, the greater feeling of security is created in the mind of the lender. The small investor should consider getting investing participants for similar reasons.

If a small investor lacks certain expertise in a particular area, he or she should seek to hook up with someone who does. For example, if your aim is to furnish money and only be the money partner, because you don't have the expertise in other areas or the desire to perform a function yourself, team up with a partner who doesn't have the money, but has expertise in maintenance, repairs, construction, management, or any other skill that a successful venture requires.

In another instance, you might have property management skills, and know someone who has repair and maintenance skills. The two of you, as partners, could team up with a money partner to buy an old 20-unit fixer-upper that you will manage and your partner will provide the necessary talent for the refurbishment and maintenance. In this way, you take advantage of the attributes of each partner to attain a common goal, which would otherwise be unattainable. It is not necessary for the partners to share profits equally. There should be some agreed recognition of the value of the services furnished by each and some procedure for equalization by distribution of profits or otherwise. Since the managing partner has to spend the time and effort to make the project a successful one, that has tremendous value that must be recognized.

Syndications have been around for years. If you have certain expertise and need investors, team up with money partners who should not be involved with other aspects of the project such as management, repairs, and maintenance. You would be surprised how many people are interested in investing in real estate solely for the purpose of receiving a higher rate of return than might otherwise be available and a share of the upside potential that real estate projects usually have.

Tips on Getting Investors

It is very hard to borrow money from friends and family, especially for your first transaction because they won't believe you know what you're doing. But once you show them a successful real estate investment you've managed, they're willing investors.

How do you improve your chances of getting others to invest with you? If you had a situation where you wanted to buy a property and you needed a $50,000 deposit. And you went to a potential investor and said, "I want you to be my partner and we have to put up a $50,000 deposit"—that's one scenario with a low probability of success.

A better scenario with a higher degree of success is: "I've already put up $50,000 to buy this property that I think has great potential. I'm offering you the opportunity to come in on the ground floor as my partner and share in the benefits." This concept is a lot easier to sell because your money is already where your mouth is. You've already displayed your confidence in the deal. It's a whole different selling situation compared with someone who is thinking of investing. It's strong because you have shown that you have faith in the transaction and don't need them to tie up the deal. It's very hard to do a transaction where the investors are asked to put up 100 percent of the money. Investors like the feeling of security that they feel when they know that the originator of the transaction has a monetary stake in the deal.

Guidelines for Real Estate Investing Partnerships

How do you get started forming a real estate investing partnership? Find a lawyer or a developer who has done something similar and pick their brains. Explain that you're a total novice and you know they're successful in real estate and your education will begin. Here are some basic guidelines for forming a partnership:

- If you are the project manager it is imperative that you have total control over all aspects of the project other than financing arrangements and sale of the project. Give as little detailed information as you can to satisfy your money partners. Investors can be intimidated by too much information, which they don't have the ability or desire to interpret. Don't get into details unless they're specifically requested. Unless you have very knowledgeable investors, only give them whatever it is in the way of information that will make them feel secure in their participation in a good investment. Give them the positives in glowing terms, and play down the negatives.
- Always have an appropriate method of periodic communication. It should be consistent and on time, such as bimonthly or twice yearly. If you promise a report every 90 days, make sure you keep your promise. Don't wait until your investors ask for it. Keep all of your partners in the loop especially if you have some good news to report.
- Make sure investors know all their obligations, such as periodic cash calls, if your project runs into problems. You don't want them to be surprised when you ask for more money.

- Include incentives. Give investors something to peak their interest. You have to assess the appetite of any party putting in money. Find out what they want. Is it primarily a guaranteed minimum fixed return, coupled with some additional return in the future when a sale or refinancing occurs? Or do they want a percentage of the upside instead?

- If you have already obtained a bank loan, your investors will be impressed that a bank looks favorably on the project and that makes it easier for them to part with some money.

- Be sure there's some reasonable divorce method if some partner wants out. The last thing anyone wants is to be forced to live with an unhappy partner. The most equitable solution I have used is one where at a given time any partner may solicit an offer for purchase of the entire project. If that partner has received an offer that he or she is willing to accept, that offer is submitted to the other partners who can either accept the offer and consent to the sale of the property or buy the interest of the partner who wants out by paying him or her what they would have received if the offer were accepted and the entire project sold.

- Write a business plan that explains the source of the expertise necessary to make the investment a winner. If you don't have a skill needed, specify who does and what it will cost. As part of the business plan, you can offer the silent investing partners several options such as a fixed percentage of the profits, or a guarantee of a minimum rate of return in lieu of a piece of the action, or any combination you wish to present.

- There has to be a significant incentive for the developer or managing partner to make the deal successful, and make him want to work for it. If you cut his interest down to a point where it's not worth his considerable effort, he will likely just say "It's not worth the time and aggravation."

Dividing Up the Investment Pie

How do you determine the best way to answer the questions about who gets what in a deal and how much should someone be paid? Find out who does these sort of things for a living, and tap their brains. Lawyers and developers in your area who have successfully handled similar situations are an ideal source of information and worth whatever fee they charge. For example, you say to the lawyer, Judy Jones, "What's typical in these kinds of deals? What kind of deal do you think can be made?" These people can guide you in structuring a deal that will fly. They can tell you how they tailored similar deals. They might say, "This is what I did last time and it worked." It's not unusual for lawyers to represent clients investing in the type of deal you're considering. In fact, it's not uncommon for a lawyer to have a client as a lender and a client who's an investor and to put them together in a transaction with the lawyer preparing all the necessary documents.

As part of my legal practice, I have often been approached by a client seeking a lender. If I was successful, I was paid a finder's fee for providing a lender, which was in addition to my fees for legal services rendered.

Another thing to remember when it comes time to invest in real estate is, "Never try to get something for nothing; always pay for it." The opposite is also true, "Never give something for nothing." If someone says to you, "I'll do it for nothing." That's probably what it's worth, nothing!

MORTGAGE ALTERNATIVES FOR SMALL INVESTORS

If you don't already own a home, you can still start investing in income properties. But first, it's important you keep this in mind: In order to qualify for owner-occupied financing, you have to honor the lender's occupancy requirement, which often means you must intend to live in the mortgaged property for at least one year. With that stipulation in mind, you can begin the wealth-building process by selecting a high loan-to-value (LTV) loan program that's most appropriate for you.

Purchase a one- to four-family property, move into it for one year, then rent it out and repeat the strategy again. Even after you move out, the owner-occupied financing remains with the property.

Getting Started: High-Leverage Loan Programs for Owner-Occupants

The following nine programs provide investors with all types of no down payment or low down payment possibilities:

1. *FHA 203(b).* This is the most popular program available through the Federal Housing Administration (FHA), a government agency that will insure real estate loans through conventional lenders. Under this program, cash-short buyers can finance one to four units with as little as 3 percent down. Currently loan limits are $333,700 on single units, $427,150 on two-family units, $516,300 on three-family units, and $641,650 on four-family units. Qualifying standards (income required and credit) are more lenient than conventional loans and those who show steady income and good-faith in paying their bills usually qualify.
2. *FHA/VA 203(v).* This program is similar to the 203 (b) except that it's offered only to qualified veterans with less of a down payment requirement.
3. *FHA 203(k).* This plan is ideal for homebuyers who want to renovate, rehab, or add more value to a property. This

two-in-one program allows you to combine a home's purchase price and renovation costs all in one mortgage.

4. *FHA qualifying assumptions.* When market interest rates are high, look for sellers with FHA mortgages originated when rates were lower. Pay the sellers for their equity (or whatever amount you negotiate) and then assume the seller's mortgage. Qualifying for this type of mortgage is a lot less complicated than originating a new loan, and you gain the benefit of acquiring a mortgage at below market interest rates.

5. *FHA/VA nonqualifying assumptions.* Prior to 1987, when the FHA and Veteran's Administration (VA) stopped making them, millions of these loans were originated. Though most of these loans have been repaid, a few sellers retained them. The nonqualifying assumable loan is the easiest and least costly loan you can get. The reason: There are no questions asked of the borrower, and all that's required is payment of a small assumption fee. See a list of repossessed VA-owned properties at their web site at www.vahomeswash.com.

6. *HUD homes.* When FHA borrowers fail to make their loan payments, the Department of Urban Development (HUD), the parent of the FHA, takes over ownership of these properties. HUD properties can be purchased with as little as 3 percent down. For more details, ask a HUD registered realtor, or see their web site at www.hud.gov.

7. *VA mortgages.* If you're an eligible veteran, you can borrow up to $240,000 with no money down to buy a home. To get the ball rolling, remit your discharge papers to the VA to get your certificate of eligibility. No-cash-to-close and ease of qualifying are two more of the benefits given to those who served honorably in the U.S. military.

8. *VA qualifying assumptions.* Existing VA loans can easily be assumed by veterans or nonveterans. When market interest rates

are high, look for sellers with VA mortgages originated when rates were lower. And just like FHA no qualifying assumptions, the VA loan is easy to qualify for and less costly than originating a new loan.

9. *Real estate owned (REO).* REO is a term commercial lenders (such as banks or savings and loans) use to describe their inventory of foreclosed real estate. A large multibranch savings and loan, for example, would have an REO department that would oversee and manage its holdings. Should a lender foreclose on a house, for instance, the owner or tenant of the house would immediately be evicted. Then, the lender (who is now the new owner), would secure it, and would eventually put it up for sale. More often than not, these properties are sold at bargain prices with great terms. Your job should be to make a thorough search of these REO managers and get a list of their inventory. You could also find out who the realtors are who make it their business to sell a lender's REO.

SUMMARY

The content of this chapter may overwhelm the small real estate investor, but don't give up. There are still fortunes both large and small to be made in real estate. Traditionally, real estate values increase at a rate equaling or exceeding inflation. Real estate is a limited commodity and each piece is unique. If you make some bad deals, remember everyone does, including Donald Trump. It is true, however, that you will learn much more from your failures than you ever will from your successes.

7

Get Help from the Best Real Estate Specialists You Can Find

Key Points

- Hire people based on their reputation and track record.
- Be willing to pay a premium.
- Play up the prestige of your professionals.
- Hiring tips for key specialties.

D ONALD TRUMP HAS many visionary ideas for his real estate investments, and he ultimately makes all the important decisions himself, but before any final decision is made, he listens very closely to the counsel and advice of experts. In every real estate project, Trump retains top real estate specialists to help him—architects, lawyers, leasing agents, accountants, contractors, engineers, designers, and others. When it comes to legal documents or business advice, he calls on me first to get my thoughts. He knows that he can accomplish much more than he ever could himself by using the services of top real estate professionals like me. This chapter describes how you can find really good people whose value to you will cover the cost of their fee many times over.

Many small investors get into trouble because they try to do everything themselves, right down to their own legal and tax work. To be successful with your real estate project, you need to get the best people in the field to help you.

For example, when I bought a radio station on Long Island with my brother-in-law, Martin Beck, I knew nothing about the radio business, but he did. He knew about ratings and how to attract more listeners. He knew about the rating sweeps and how to increase your advertising revenue. He had worked for an advertising agency selling radio time, and he knew how advertisers thought, and the best way to package what we were planning to sell. He also knew a lot about cost saving. For example, you don't need an individual newscaster for six radio stations. You can tie in with CNN News and use their news for all stations with minor changes based on locality. Previously, you needed to staff a separate news department. With Marty's industry expertise, and my financing and business acumen, we created a very successful business that was ultimately sold for a profit of millions of dollars. Don't think you can do everything yourself. Surround yourself with professionals and you'll save yourself aggravation and even money.

INVESTING CASE STUDY

VILLA TRUMP BRAZIL

Trump has earned such a reputation for hiring top people, and creating quality and luxury in whatever he does, that he can now license his brand and property design and management expertise to other real estate investors. They realize the value of having a top name (in this case, Trump) associated with their development. They appreciate the marketing power it gives them. (I'll describe later in the chapter how small investors can use the same principle when hiring architects, builders, and designers.) One example of this is a project near Sao Paulo, called Villa Trump Brazil. For Trump to permit his name to be connected with this project, the land owners paid him $1 million cash up front, plus a share of the profits on anything over $45 million in sales. They intend to sell 400 building lots at $300,000 each. That's $120 million in sales right there. Except for supervision and guidance, Trump's input is minimal with no dollars in but he'll get lots of dollars out. His major contribution is his name coupled with his expertise in development supervision. It will inevitably turn out to be a beautiful, luxurious first-class development. It's a huge project on 1659 acres, including a Jack Nicklaus signature golf course and golf academy, with a nine-hole executive course for the academy. It will feature a high-quality boutique hotel, situated around the 18-hole golf course along with 18 mansions, worth between $4 and $10 million.

Trump wouldn't ordinarily go out and build a project in Sao Paulo, Brazil. However, local real estate developers knew that there were many wealthy Brazilians who would pay more for the quality and luxury Trump represents. The group of savvy visionaries said, "We'll do the work. We'll put up the money, build it, and we'll give you a share of the profits. We need to use the Trump name and we want to utilize your expertise in selling the units and running the facility, and furnishing the services available from your staff of experts." The key to Trump's approval was their consent that the project will be subject to the complete control by Trump's organization. We control what it looks like. We control what they do and how they do it. The price of using the Trump name is that every project has to meet the rigid Trump standard of excellence.

HIRE PEOPLE BASED ON THEIR REPUTATION AND TRACK RECORD

When it comes to specialty areas of real estate like law or design or contracting, you want to avoid someone who just occasionally dabbles in the real estate field, like your neighbor's brother. You want a professional who makes a living in the real estate specialty you need.

How do you find good real estate professionals? Start by keeping an eye out for examples of work you admire, such as a local landscape or building renovation, then find out who the designer or contractor was. Also, contact lawyers and contractors that you know have done work on projects like yours, and who will likely do good, quality work for you. It is especially important, for example, if you have a zoning problem, that you hire a local zoning lawyer who is well versed in zoning matters and has the political connections to get things done.

You always want to use full-time specialists in their field of endeavor, not part-timers. They won't be up-to-date on the latest techniques. Their fees will probably be less than the best in the field, but they won't have the knowledge you need. Every real estate parcel has problems of one kind or another that will require the expertise of a specialist. Keep in mind, too, that part-time people will only give you a part-time effort.

Another consideration is giving preference to local people—try not to bring in people from outside unless they are really outstanding. Locals will be better informed about the area and will have better connections with the contractors and other people that you will need.

The best method of identifying quality professionals is to speak to another investor/renovator/builder who is doing what you want to do and get recommendations. Be aware however, they may not want to talk to or be honest with you if they feel you're a competitor. If they are not helpful, the information you seek may be available from their lawyer, realtor, or broker who can probably get you the information you're seeking. They will gladly cooperate if they think you're a potential client.

Let the Realtor Be Your Guide

The experienced local real estate agent is your best source of information. You want a realtor who has an outstanding record dealing with the kind of property you are investing in and in the location you have interest in. Real estate agents also are great networkers with other key specialists in the real estate industry. If, for example, you see an apartment building with exquisite landscaping, make inquiries about the name of the realtor or broker who handled the latest sale of the property. They either know who did the landscaping, or they can get the information from their client.

The key is to elicit the realtor's full cooperation by holding out the likelihood that you'll use him in your real estate matters. You may or may not decide to use him in the long run, but you should at least initially seduce him by exhibiting your good intentions. Explain why you need the information, and he will often jump to get you everything that you need, especially if he thinks you are serious about buying a property. Moreover, depending on the size of the brokerage office, he will likely have a great deal of valuable information stored in his database. He can tell you who the owner of a beautiful new property is, how much he paid for the property, what it cost to build, and who the general contractor (GC) was, and if he doesn't have this data, he can get it. He can call any former client and say, "I have a client that likes very much what you built. Who did you use as a GC?"

Then get the name of the GC or architect and say to him, "You did such and such a job and it really looks good, we would like to use you for our project. Can I see your portfolio?"

You need to make a connection with someone who has done an outstanding job on the same type of work you need done. The best contact to get you started is the local realtor in the area. Don't limit yourself to just one. Go to two or three realtors and get as much information as you can. Ask a whole bunch of questions. Then, if the same name keeps popping up again and again for a given specialty, that's probably the one to use.

BE WILLING TO PAY A PREMIUM

Generally speaking, it's worth it to pay for the best people in their real estate specialty since they have the ability to significantly add value to your investment. Trump's budget for any project usually assumes that he will hire the best people in every area of his real estate business. Small investors have smaller budgets to work with and should focus their spending on the few people who are deemed to be essential to the success of the project. If you have a property with a complicated tax situation, a top tax accountant may be a good investment, at least for the first year. If you are buying a fixer-upper, you should hire an interior designer, architect, and landscape architect. If you are smart about how you use them, the value they add to your project can far outweigh any fee they charge. If you are an investor with limited funds, think about giving your professionals a small piece of the profits after you've recouped all your expenses. If they think they're working for themselves, they'll do an even better job.

PLAY UP THE PRESTIGE OF YOUR PROFESSIONALS

If you hire a designer or builder who has name recognition with potential buyers or tenants, or who has built well-known buildings they would be familiar with, use that information as part of your marketing message for the property. Play up the prestige of the architect, interior designer, contractor, landscape architect, or other professional. This is one way you can recoup the extra money you spent hiring a big name professional. If you hire a designer who is well known, or who has worked on fine buildings that your buyers are familiar with, this is powerful "sizzle" and will definitely get your customers' attention. For example, Trump used Costas Kondylis as his architect for the Trump World Tower, because Kondylis had earned a great deal of recognition and prestige for his design of high-priced condominium units.

All of the literature relating to the Trump National Golf Club in Palm Beach recites that it is a Jim Fazio course, a name well-known and respected in golf course design. All of the literature relating to the Grand Hyatt Hotel boasted that Der Scutt, a name synonymous with creativity, was the architect redesigning the old Commodore Hotel building.

HIRING TIPS FOR KEY SPECIALTIES

Hiring a Building Architect or Landscape Architect

1. Be certain that the architect you hire is neither too big nor too small for the project you are planning. Let them justify why you should use them.

2. Try to get a preliminary rendering before you commit dollars.

3. Negotiate all fees in advance and get it in writing.

4. Try to get a fixed fee rather than time charges. If you agree to time charges get a list of the hourly wage rate of everyone who will be working on your project.

5. Get an estimate of all costs for which you're responsible.

6. Meet everyone who will be working on your account and understand what function each will perform.

7. Negotiate a quick and painless procedure for terminating the relationship if you're unhappy with it.

8. Get the right to any work product they created while you paid for it.

Questions You Should Ask before Hiring Anyone

- What other jobs are you working on at this time?
- When will you start the assignment? When will you finish it?
- When can I get a preliminary rendering to approve?
- What other builders have you worked for recently?
- How long have you been in business?
- How many people do you employ?

Hiring a Contractor

1. Make sure they are licensed, bonded, and employ union labor, if it's necessary.

2. Check their references.

3. Check their availability and number of employees available to do your job.

4. Check with the local business bureau or local municipal office where complaints may be lodged.

5. Try to inspect their place of business. If it's sloppy, their work will probably be sloppy also and probably take more time.

6. If at all possible, negotiate a fixed price contract.

7. Get everything in writing. Beware of standard forms with small print on the back. Usually what the big print "giveth" the small print "taketh" away.

8. If the size of the job warrants it, find out if the contractor is bondable and how much more the job will cost if the contractor is required to post a bond to ensure his performance.

Questions You Should Ask before Hiring a Contractor

- Ask the same questions you would ask when hiring an architect or a landscape designer plus the following additional questions.
- Will you give me a contract with a price specifying my maximum liability?
- How much liability insurance do you carry for personal injury or property damage?
- Who's your insurance carrier?
- Do you have any pending lawsuits to which you are a party?
- What was your last job?

Hiring a Real Estate Agent

1. Get an agent close to your property who is properly sized to service your needs.

2. Meet all the people who will be working on your account.

3. Check the local real estate board for any information or complaints.

4. Find out what their rates are and what services they will perform.

5. Get examples of the kind of reports they will furnish to you about your property.

6. Find out how inquiries as well as complaints are handled by the agent.

Questions You Should Ask before Hiring a Real Estate Agent

- What other owners do you presently represent?
- Are you the agent for other buildings comparable to mine?

- If so, how many, for how long, and where are they?
- What advertising will you do for my property?

Hiring an Attorney or Accountant

1. Only hire someone experienced in real estate projects similar to the one you are contemplating.
2. Unless you have a complicated deal, stay away from large law firms. Their fees usually match their size and you'll get lost in the shuffle. You'll do better with a smaller firm where you can establish a good rapport with the individual servicing your needs.
3. Agree on a fee structure in advance. Don't be embarrassed to negotiate for a lower fee. Explain that you're just starting out and have a limited budget to work with.
4. Get a list of clients in the business of real estate that they represent and call a few for references.
5. Before hiring a lawyer, check with the bar association to ascertain if the lawyer is in good standing with an unblemished record.
6. Make sure any accountant you hire is a CPA.
7. If you don't feel "warm and cozy" after meeting with any professional, look farther.

The same questions you would ask before hiring other professionals are generally applicable to lawyers and accountants.

8

WHY TRUMP BUILDING PROJECTS ARE ALWAYS ON TIME AND UNDER BUDGET

KEY POINTS

- Manage contractors and control costs.
- Be your own general contractor when possible.
- Create incentives for being early rather than having penalties for being late.
- Be fanatical about details.
- Motivate people.

DONALD TRUMP LEARNED most of what he knows about the construction business from his father, who was also a renowned real estate developer and builder. One of the earliest photos of Donald shows him at the age of 12 inspecting the foundation of one of his father's buildings. Fred Trump was meticulous in overseeing what he built. He was very involved and insisted on knowing every detail of how his buildings were being constructed, from laying bricks and installing steel beams to digging foundations, until the building was completed. Donald inherited his father's work ethic. A classic example of Donald Trump's hands-on monitoring of construction progress occurred when he was transforming the old Briar Hall golf course into what is now Trump National Golf and Country Club in Briarcliff Manor, New York. While inspecting the site, he learned that a huge amount of granite existed at a critical spot and would require a major amount of blasting to remove. Trump was curious and went to the spot and said, "Why can't we incorporate the stone to serve as a backdrop for a major waterfall on a golf hole?" The site engineer replied, "You're talking about a waterfall that will be over 100 feet high and will require a large source of water to make it eye catching. It's going to cost millions to build." Trump said, "I know, but it will be my signature hole and everyone who plays the course will talk about it. It's worth the price." Trump was right. The 13th hole at Trump National is the "wow" hole on the entire course.

MANAGE CONTRACTORS AND CONTROL COSTS

Small investors who closely monitor the progress and problems that arise in their own building and renovation projects will find many similar opportunities to make unexpected improvements or cost savings. Like Trump, you need to learn as much as you can about every aspect of the real estate business and construction. The more knowledge you have about prices, costs, options, materials, real estate services, and other factors, the more opportunities you have to reduce costs and increase profits.

You can learn a great deal by staying in close communication with the specialists you hire to work on your project, and encourage them to speak their minds. Since you should only hire people with a proven capabilities, listen to their advice but remember the final decision should be yours. For example, I recommend you employ a good architect to design plans and specifications. Every good architect is a source of valuable real estate information but also has access to reliable general contractors (GCs) and the various trades used by other clients. This is a great source of valuable contacts for you to investigate. Find out who has built a building similar to the one you are contemplating and learn who was used as the GC. Call that GC and tell him of your desire to build a building and you're considering him or his firm for the job. You'll undoubtedly get a list of the jobs for which he acted as GC and the names of the owners. Get as much information as you can as to the anticipated costs, time for construction, and fees to be paid. Tell the GC that you'll get back to him and then check him out. Check the workmanship of the buildings for which he or his firm was the GC. Speak to the owners of those buildings in a face-to-face meeting to find out the plusses and minuses of the GC. Was he accurate in forecasting the budget? Was the job finished on time, if not, why not? What were the names of the subcontractors who were employed for the various trades? How good were they? Would you use them again? If you assemble the same information from multiple sources, you're on your way to creating your own data base for future reference.

BE YOUR OWN GENERAL CONTRACTOR
WHEN POSSIBLE

In a typical situation, a GC is hired to oversee all of the work. He will build the structure and he will contract with all the necessary trades to complete the construction at a total price. If you are inexperienced in the many facets of construction, hiring a GC is the way to go even though it may cost more. Donald Trump, on occasion, hires a GC, but usually hires a construction manager (CM). The basic difference between a GC and a CM is in the responsibility for picking and hiring subcontractors and negotiating their contracts. If a GC gives you a total price, he will hire all of the subcontractors to do each aspect of the work. The GC builds his profit into the total price. A CM usually gets a fee that is a percentage based on the total cost of construction. The CM acts as the owner's representative and he's responsible for getting the architect and engineers to do the plans and specifications and gets bids from contractors for the various trades. When bids are received, they are submitted to the owner who then decides which contractors to use and what amount will be paid for the work. By using a CM instead of a GC, Trump controls the bidding and also controls who will be the contractor for each trade. He can choose the ones he likes. If he uses a GC, the GC goes out and gets the bids. The GC gets to pick and choose the contractors because he has total responsibility for the construction. He hires the subcontractors and pays them from the monies received from Trump.

Every GC will always build in a profit margin and a reserve for contingencies on the possibility that the subcontractors won't come in at the prices he has in mind or some unseen problem will occur during the course of construction. The quandry is, you will never know if the reserve (the contingency) is too much or too little until the job is completed. If the reserve was too high, you overpaid. If it was too low, the GC's profit disintegrates. If it virtually disappears, the GC may either run into financial trouble or elect not to finish the job. This will undoubtedly result in considerable aggravation, if not litigation, for you. The GC may come back to you and say something like: "Look, I projected my steel to cost $20,000, but steel prices went up and it came in at $31,000." Ordinarily, you might want to reply, "Well, that's your problem, not mine." But if you have a GC in financial trouble, you're not going to get the job finished on time or with the same level of craftsmanship you expect. He's going to figure out some way to control his losses.

To avoid major pitfalls, Trump considers a CM as the better way to go. The CM usually has good contacts with all the trades and usually knows the best ones to do most of the work. Therefore, he might say to Trump, "I have three electrical contractors that I've worked with before and are qualified to bid on the electrical work for the building." If Trump gives the CM the go ahead, the acceptable contractors submit their bids. The CM may recommend which bid to accept, and it doesn't necessarily have to be the lowest one. The CM does this with all the trades, so he creates a *trade breakdown* (i.e., a spreadsheet listing all of the trades that will perform each aspect of work on the building). Then Trump will go through all these trades and will either, "approve, or disapprove" often saying, "Yes, I've used this guy before, he's good." Or, Trump may personally get involved, as he usually does, and speak to the contractors directly and negotiate the pricing. Once the trades are in place, the CM is responsible for seeing that everything goes according to schedule. The role of the CM is the same regardless of the size of the building or the cost of construction or renovation.

It should be noted that a GC may be hired on a "cost plus" basis. That means that the GC will solicit bids from contractors, negotiate them for you, and supervise the construction. You will sign all of the contacts with the various trades and will be responsible for all payments. The GC's profit is computed as a certain percentage of the costs (typically 1% to 4% depending on the size of the project—the larger the project the lower the percentage).

CREATE INCENTIVES FOR BEING EARLY RATHER THAN HAVING PENALTIES FOR BEING LATE

There are usually delays in any construction that are unforeseen. However, if a contractor knows that if he finishes before a certain date he gets a bonus, he will move heaven and earth to earn that bonus, so if there is a delay, he will figure out how to work around it. Maybe they'll put in overtime, or maybe they'll just make every effort to get the job done early.

Instead of getting into an argument with a contractor, such as, "You said you were going to complete this building in December, and now it's January and you're nowhere near completion. You agreed that you would pay a penalty for every day you're late past December except for delays for causes beyond your control. I'm going to insist on the penalty." With that scenario, all that happens is that the contractor comes up with a list of all the things beyond his control that caused delays. So, at best, you end up in a dispute with the contractor, which ultimately has to be resolved by negotiation or litigation. The contractor is unhappy knowing his profit is diminished or wiped out entirely. So you would be dealing with an unhappy contractor contrasted with a happy contractor who has an opportunity to make an even greater profit by finishing early. By far the worst thing that can happen is that a contractor walks off the job. In addition to the inevitable delay, the costs incurred in hiring someone new can be astronomical. Any "savior" knows you're in a bind and will charge a premium to bail you out. You will be told how much more it will cost to correct the work done by the departing contractor. Try to keep your contractor and all subcontractors working on the job if it's at all possible. If, however, you find that you hired a bad apple, line up a suitable replacement before the need arises.

If a contractor gives Trump a bid of $100,000, Trump may say "no way, but I will give you $60,000," and they will argue over the amount, and maybe ultimately agree on $70,000. Then Trump will say, "I'll tell you what I'll do, if you complete the work early, I'll give you an additional $500 for every day you finish before the 90 days we agreed on. But the maximum I'll pay you is $85,000." Initially the guy wanted $100,000, agreed to $70,000, but now has a chance to earn $85,000. He will work his tail off to earn as much of the extra $15,000 as he can.

Construction Speed Is Valuable

When you're dealing with contractors, you want them to finish ASAP. Every property has fixed expenses such as taxes, insurance, interest on loans, and other items, and these costs don't go away during the time of construction when your building is non-income producing. The sooner your project is completed and you are able to start receiving income, either by renting or selling the property, or part of it, the better off you are. If you compute how much it costs per diem to carry the property you can offer contractors an early-completion bonus based on this figure, but the total is still less than you would have paid if they adhered to a regular construction schedule. This creates a win-win situation that Trump has used successfully over and over again. For example, on Trump World Tower, the daily carrying cost for invested or borrowed money, taxes, insurance, and other expenses exceeded $80,000 a day! By creating incentive arrangements on negotiated contracts, Trump started closing the sale of units more than 90 days ahead of schedule, a saving in excess of $10 million. While the projects a small real estate investor undertakes involve much less money, the potential savings are still significant. If you analyze the loss of income on your investment and the interest on borrowed funds and taxes and other expenses, which accrue during the period of construction or renovation, you will be amazed at the per diem loss you suffer. Anything you can do to reduce the period of loss is a win.

The Critical Path

One of the things that Trump and all GCs and CMs do is to create what is known as a *critical path*. A critical path is a timeline that indicates when various components of the project are going to be started and completed. The critical path reflects the entire building process, from the time ground is broken until the building is completed. It takes into account all the component parts. For instance, let's say you're constructing a building and you plan to start excavation on May 1, but you may have to demolish an existing structure before you can excavate. So you would schedule March 1 as the demolition start date, and you block out two months that you believe will be adequate to complete the demolition. Next you estimate how long excavation will take and block that time out. Then you have to figure out when you can start pouring the concrete foundations and how long that will take. Then setting the steel for the structure can begin. Once the steel is set, you have to anticipate how many floors can be done while the steel is going up, until you finally top off the building. Synchronized with topping off the building is the construction of the facade (curtain wall) on the lower level. Eventually you have to start doing the interior installations that involve the heating systems, the ventilating systems, and the elevators. The critical path depicts when each piece is anticipated to start and end. If one element is late, which often happens, it could affect the whole schedule because some items cannot be started until others are completed. It is the job of the CM to be at the construction site every day to monitor progress and to make periodic reports to Trump. Notwithstanding the periodic reports from the CM, Trump constantly visits each of his construction sites to satisfy himself that the timeline is being adhered to and the construction will be completed on or before the scheduled completion date.

BE FANATICAL ABOUT DETAILS

If you want the job to be finished on time, you (and your CM if you have one), have to ascertain that all of the many details will conform to their allotted time. This is all about supervision of the various contracting trades as they perform their work. Unless there is careful coordination, problems will occur. For example, painting usually has to be done before a final floor is laid. If the painting was done but it was a bad job, it may have to be redone. Unless it happens before the flooring is finished, correction could damage the flooring. If someone doesn't push the painter to correct his shoddy work quickly, and the new floor is laid without a protective plastic coating before the corrective work is done, it may be damaged by paint spots. If that happens the flooring may require repair, an an additional expense that better coordination could have avoided.

The main thing to remember is that you or your CM have to point out construction deficiencies early so that they don't affect something else that is imminent, and force a delay or repair that could have been avoided. Here's another example: Suppose your job calls for installation of a marble floor and you notice that a number of the marble slabs are cracked. That marble has to be replaced right away, but what if you don't have matching replacement slabs, or the quarry doesn't have them either? How do you replace four slabs of cracked marble that originally matched with pieces that don't match? You can't and the only feasible solution is to tear up the whole floor! The sooner you realize you have a major problem like this, the better. A good pair of eyes can save you a lot of money and hours of aggravation.

When Donald Trump decided to install a magnificent green marble floor in the GM Building, he had all the marble that would be needed plus some extra slabs shipped to New York from Italy. The quarry was also instructed to keep a quantity of slabs on reserve at the quarry should they be needed. Because the amount of marble to be used was extensive, the quarry was willing to comply to get the order. Before the laying of the floor was started, each crate was opened and each piece of marble inside was inspected by hand to see that it matched the other slabs and had no imperfections or damage. If any of these defects were found, the slab was discarded. This painstaking procedure enabled the entire floor to be laid in record time with a minimum of inconvenience to the tenants. With careful foresight and planning, you too can avoid problems that would otherwise occur. It's worth the additional time and effort.

MOTIVATE PEOPLE

One of Donald Trump's greatest attributes is his willingness to bestow praise on someone in the presence of others. He has often introduced me as the best real estate lawyer in New York City or the State of New York or the United States depending on whom he's trying to impress at the time. I know how good I am but I still like to hear him say it. Donald does the same thing with janitors, cleaning people, handymen, and others who are a part of the overall Trump operation. He is cordial and friendly with the people who work for him regardless of their job. He will often take the time to be in a photo with someone realizing that it might make his or her day. When Trump visits a job site and he sees a laborer or a contractor working hard or doing a good job, he will complement that person and the work he is doing. I have visited a construction site with Donald and he'd stop and say, "George, see that woodwork? This guy is the best wood-worker in the entire city, maybe the world." I knew that that was exaggerated praise but the broad smile on the worker's face said it all. He will tell his friends and family what Trump said and you can be sure he will be a perfectionist in everything he does for Trump.

You can motivate your real estate specialists like Trump. For example, if someone is painting your house. You walk by and say, "Hey, that really looks good; you're really doing a great job." What did it cost you? Nothing! You can be sure that the worker will do a better job as a result of your praise. This is how Trump inspires people. On the other hand, you could go by the house and say to the painter, "Hey, why are you taking so long to do that?" Now you have taken a negative approach, and he has to defend his position. If he feels unappreciated his work will reflect his attitude.

Trump also motivates contractors by staying in touch with them personally. When Trump is negotiating over the phone with contractors about a job, he will speak personally to them, he won't have someone else do it. When bidding out any contracts he gets a list of all the trades, and he will personally call each of them and negotiate the final price. This takes place after his people have already negotiated prices and have come up with a price acceptable to the contractor. When the time for finalization has arrived, Trump calls and gives the final push. "I'd like to do the deal with you because I love your work, but I can't. Your numbers are way out of line. You bid $1,000, I have a bid for $600; aren't you ashamed to be that far off?" "But I do better work," is often the reply. Trump responds, "I only deal with people who do great work but your bid is $400 more than my other bid from another guy I've used before and I guess he wants the job more than you do. You have to do something for me to make this work." Usually an agreement is reached which is mutually acceptable. Donald will often end it with, "I know I'm still overpaying but I know you'll do a great job. Don't let me down." Trump will often say, "This guy charges more, but he does a better job, and he's the one I'm going to hire even though he's not the lowest bidder."

The main point for you to remember is that there is inherent value in fostering and maintaining good relationships with your agent, contractors, tenants, and everyone else involved in your real estate investing business directly or incidentally. It doesn't cost you anything if you do it, but it will cost you a bundle of money if you don't. Whenever possible, cultivate all relationships personally. A compliment or friendly word or gesture from you has special meaning. The same thing coming from an associate of yours is given much less value in the mind of the recipient.

9

TRUMP MARKETING STRATEGIES

Selling the "Sizzle" Sells the Product

KEY POINTS

- How selling the "sizzle" sells the product.
- Showing the property: The aesthetics must draw people in.
- Use dazzling presentations.
- Advertising strategies.
- Use intelligent promotions.
- Marketing to home buyers and renters.

IF YOU HAVE adopted some of Trump's strategies that I described in earlier chapters, then you have designed into your property some features that will dazzle your buyers or tenants albeit in a lesser way than the seven-story marble waterfall in the atrium of Trump Tower. Maybe you built a rose-covered arbor over the entrance to your rental property, or you installed marble tile and a Jacuzzi tub in the bathrooms. Once you have finished designing and building some eye-catching features into a property, it's time to focus on marketing the property to buyers and tenants. Now you can put to work those great attention-getting methods that will make people willing to pay more for your property and buy it or rent it quickly. This chapter describes some of the key marketing strategies Trump uses to communicate the value, excitement, and appeal of his properties to potential buyers or tenants.

How Selling the "Sizzle" Sells the Product

I believe the "sizzle" idea in marketing originally came from Chinese restaurants. They served one of their beef or seafood dishes in a hot iron skillet that sizzled so delectably that it would make their customer's mouth water and had the same effect on everyone who heard the sound. The dish became more appetizing just because of the sizzle. The same concept applies to real estate. Your customers have a lot of choices before they decide on a property, and many of the features of your property will be similar to those of your competition. You need to find ways to make your property appear to be more than a plain vanilla commodity by effectively communicating to the potential customer the exclusivity and superiority of your product. Trump is master at finding clever ways to use showmanship to create the sizzle for his properties.

I recommend that you make a list of all the features about your property that distinguish it from your competition. You may even want to create an eye-catching flyer that you can give to prospective buyers or tenants describing these features in detail. When you are showing the property, these are the elements that you want to play up and emphasize. Make sure that everyone who sees the property sees each of these features. For example, if you hired a landscape designer to work on the property, you might give each person who tours the property a fresh cut flower from the garden to play up this aspect of the property's sizzle. If you have hired an architect, interior designer, or contractor to work on the property, you might invite him to your open house so he can describe their work to prospective customers, and what he did on your property to make it special. Consider making a video presentation of him describing his work and have it running when you show the property. A display board indicating the textures of carpeting, the color of finished woodwork, or the material used for countertops, as well as other materials is a good visual selling tool.

Model homes or model rooms are very effective visual aids for home sales. By using a skillful, creative interior designer the home or room can be tastefully decorated for maximum eye appeal. The key is to get the customer to think, "I can see myself living here." It's a good idea to install better materials in your models and prices of these "extras" should be readily available and what is considered "building standard" should be explained to any prospect who seems to be interested in cost saving.

If Trump is building multimillion dollar houses, he will build one or two model homes that will be carefully, lavishly, and intelligently equipped in every detail. If one bedroom is a little undersized, the furniture in it will be smaller to make the room seem larger. If a particular room has a lack of natural light, the room colors and the carpeting will be light colors to help correct the deficiency. Where ceiling height is a selling point, decorative moldings and lighting fixtures will be installed to accent the additional height. When Trump builds an apartment building, the lobby entrance is always an eye-catcher. You will see pictures of this elaborate lobby together with the highlights of other amenities in the brochures or other selling tools that are given to the potential customer. The brochures themselves are expensive works of art that reek of money. The size and quality of all literature creates the impression of distinctive exclusivity that is the Trump hallmark. Don't think of mimicking what Trump does unless you're catering to the same market. Tailor your selling tools to the best you can obtain within the limitations of your budget.

How to Play Up Your Location

Every piece of real estate is unique and has a specific location that has both positives and negatives. I suggest you prepare a detailed list of both, and craft answers to questions your customers will ask that accentuate the positives and minimize the negatives. Here are a few examples of what I mean:

- The proximity of your site to mass transportation should be disclosed. You or your literature should say, "three blocks away" or "within walking distance" or "10 minutes from the train station," whatever seems most desirable. If the mass transportation is not a selling point, say nothing.
- If your customer is a family with children, you or your literature should indicate the proximity of schools to your site. If the school district has a high reputation, say so. If not, say nothing.

- Shopping convenience is always important to customers. If your property is near a major mall, push that point and identify some of the stores in the mall. If not, state that there are stores either nearby or in the area, whichever you feel more comfortable with.
- If you think places of worship are worth mentioning, do so. If not, you should know how far away they are and what religious affiliation they have.
- Public parks and playgrounds are another thing to stress, if it's helpful.
- Be sure you know the amount of taxes your buyer will face. If the amount is below many other localities, play that up. Otherwise, stay away from the topic until you are required to answer a direct question.

SHOWING THE PROPERTY: THE AESTHETICS MUST DRAW PEOPLE IN

Even small investors should seriously consider hiring an interior designer to prepare a property for showing. The aesthetics of showing a property are that important, and it's true in almost any kind of real estate. If I own a restaurant, I have to ask myself, "What does the restaurant have to look like that will make it attractive?" That's first, because I have to get people into the restaurant. The next thing is, now that they're in what does it look like. Would I spend extra money in the kitchen? Not unless I want patrons to see the kitchen. The money should be spent on the décor, the booths, and the tables to make the restaurant appealing. It goes without saying that everything should be clean and well maintained. Does it appeal to families? When it comes to dining out, the parents say *when*, but the children say *where*.

If you intend to attract children, think about installing swings and playground equipment. If you decide to go that route, put them in a place on your property that is readily visible. Once again, it depends on who you're trying to attract. If you are marketing to retirees or senior citizens, you need a different approach (though you might consider creating an attractive place for them to entertain their grandchildren).

If I'm renting apartments in a four-story building, I can enhance the landscaping around the entrance to get people to come in. As I have said many times before, landscape design is a critical part of the marketing sizzle of any property, because the first step with aesthetics is to get the customer to be pleased with their first visual impression, which is often the landscaping. When you have accomplished that, go on to the next step. You have them conditioned for something special and then they walk through the front door, now you have to have something appealing that matches the promise of the landscaping. Trump typically creates a total experience for the customer who is interested in one of his properties, including a tour of the property or a model/showcase, which includes a pleasant visual experience, as well as print materials, artwork, a scale model, and so on.

USE DAZZLING PRESENTATIONS

In addition to showing the property, you need to create presentation materials that help extoll the features of your property. The most dazzling presentation I ever witnessed was one performed by the Hines Company for a unique office building they were building in New York City. The building was an elliptical high-rise structure totally encased within a pink marble facade. New Yorkers promptly christened it "The Lipstick Building" because it resembled a huge tube of lipstick. Prospective tenants and space planners were skeptical that efficient office space could be constructed in an oval-shaped building. Since I represented potential tenants, I was invited to a presentation by the owner to allay any concerns I might have relating to that problem. I was escorted into a carpeted room that was beautifully furnished with plush theater-style seating that circled a raised platform in the center. After I was seated, the lights dimmed except for a spotlight on the center platform. Background music began building up to a crescendo simultaneously with the opening of the center of the raised platform and the slow emergence of a huge, elaborate scale model of the entire building. The model was lit from the interior and was far superior to any detailed replica I had ever seen. I am certain it must have cost more than $100,000 to produce. It was awe inspiring. From the time the lights dimmed until the presentation was over, a narrator extolled the virtues of the building giving a well-conceived and executed sales pitch to entice tenants to lease space. To answer the unasked question about creating efficient office layouts, part of the building opened up to show detailed office layouts complete with fixtures, furniture, office equipment, and models of people working in an extremely pleasant environment. Then the Hines narrator threw out what appeared to be the clincher. He said, "And all this can be yours for a rent of $12 a square foot." Since at that time the rental rate for most of the comparable buildings in the area was twice that amount, and based on my knowledge of construction and land acquisition costs, I knew that couldn't be the whole story. Most office leases in New York City contain a provision that the tenant will pay the landlord a proportionate share of any increase in real estate taxes and operating expenses over the amount paid by landlord for those items in the year the term of the lease commenced. I found out later that the leases for the Lipstick Building provided that tenants would pay their share of taxes and operating expenses whatever those amounts were. This created an additional cost to the tenant between $12 to $14 a square foot and the total cost of occupancy was really in the same ballpark as the competition. Even though the owner pitched prospective tenants a curveball, the $12 square foot rental got their attention.

I'm not suggesting that any small real estate owner spend more money on a presentation than is warranted by the scope of the project. Having said that, your presentation should be created to "wow" the intended customers and get them to seriously consider your product.

Video and Computer-Based Presentations

Computer-based video or slide presentations can be superb selling tools. I can see you thinking to yourself, "Yeh, but they must be expensive." The cost depends on how extensive and detailed you want them to be. At the high end, you can create a web site or interactive computer software that enables a tenant to view an apartment or office space from several different angles and see what can be seen from every window. Room sizes and rental rates can also be displayed appropriately. At the low end, a Microsoft powerpoint presentation showing different parts of the property and highlighting some attributes, works wonders. Such a presentation is not expensive and it's easy to find professionals who can create exactly what you desire at a price you can live with. One of the major advantages of such a presentation is its portability. All you need is a laptop and you're anywhere you want to be, whether it's a home, office, or meeting room. Many people pitching me as Donald Trump's business advisor have used laptop presentations very effectively. Good graphics usually capture my attention.

I would be remiss if I didn't talk about video and film presentations. A high-quality, professionally crafted film or videotape with a well-conceived script and visual effects can be an excellent selling tool. The expense of creating it varies depending upon who you hire to do the work and what you want to create. The size of your project, the nature of customer you're targeting, and the amount of your budget should be carefully considered. It's your call—do what you want and spend whatever you think is appropriate.

In my experience, film and videotaped presentations have several drawbacks and their use requires additional thought. The drawbacks are as follows:

1. The audience must be told how long the film will be and they have to be seated in one place and remain there for the duration of the film. People are reluctant to spend time watching something that may prove to be of little interest to them.
2. The audience cannot ask questions in the middle of the presentation without interrupting the flow.
3. It requires a TV monitor or a screen to be effective—that limits portability.
4. Once it is created and edited, it's difficult to add or change things at a later date and having those changes or additions made could be costly.

Despite these limitations, video and film can have a place in creating sizzle for your buyers or tenants. Just be aware of these limitations.

Literature, Artwork, and Models

Quality literature with superior graphics is an absolute necessity as a selling tool. Be sure that it displays the most prominent features of your property on the front together with some intriguing language or a slogan such as, "You've seen the rest, now view the best."

Create your own catch phrase or, better yet, have all your literature prepared by an advertising firm that specializes in real estate brochures and sales literature. The "buzz" that they can create far exceeds the cost of bringing them on board. An advertising firm can also prepare large pictures, posters, or elegant artwork to be prominently displayed in and around your sales office. It is true that, "One picture is worth a thousand words." All your visuals, photographs, and artwork reflect the level of quality you're trying to portray. You can also dazzle your customers by creating a beautiful scale model of your project. Models are most effective when your property is a development of many houses or buildings. A model showing the location of all buildings, roads, and service areas can be very informative and useful.

ADVERTISING STRATEGIES

Advertising is a necessity for most real estate, but be smart about it. Any advertisement you place should only be placed in publications that cater to the audience you're trying to reach. For example, you'll never see an ad for a Trump building in the *New York Daily News* or in the *New York Post*. The vast majority of the readers of those publications are not candidates to purchase a high priced unit in a Trump project. Occasionally, Trump will place a full page ad in the weekend magazine section of the *New York Times*. He will negotiate for a strategic location where the ad will most readily be seen by the customer he's trying to reach. More often, however, the advertising Trump places in the *New York Times* will be a tasteful full-color ad small enough to be cost-effective but large enough to be seen be the readers. If the *New York Times* or the *Wall Street Journal* prints a special real estate section, Trump often opts to display multiple ads of Trump properties in that special section and negotiates a reduced price because of the quantity of space he's purchasing. Any advertising of Trump properties in weekday editions is fairly Spartan in size and content since it is primarily intended to keep the Trump name in the public eye and to attract a customer who has an immediate need for a specific apartment. Find out what publications your target audience reads and you'll get the biggest bang for your buck.

USE INTELLIGENT PROMOTIONS

Promotions are typically used by large builders and real estate investors who have big marketing budgets. For example, if you're selling exclusive homes on a private golf course, offer a free round of golf to get folks to the golf course so they'll buy a membership to the club and can glimpse the nearby one-family homes that are selling for $3 million or more strategically situated along the course. If I were promoting a restaurant, I might give you two meals for the price of one but that doesn't work for real estate which is always a big ticket item.

However, there are many creative ways that small investors can use promotions effectively. For example, have a launch party and invite the people who might help you sell the property—real estate brokers and sales agents—to let them know what is available and how much commission they can make by participating in sales or rentals. If you don't broadcast and promote what it is you have to sell or what it is you're trying to do, you will be unsuccessful in attracting customers.

If you decide to put a sign on the property, don't make it a typical "for sale" sign. Make it more artistic than any other sign you've seen, with more information, open house times, and so on.

MARKETING TO HOME BUYERS AND RENTERS

By far the best strategy for marketing to home buyers is a friendly, knowledgeable sales agent. If you, as the owner, have those attributes, there is nothing wrong with being your own selling representative. If you need help, don't skimp when it comes to hiring a quality salesperson or broker who can exude enthusiasm for your product. Make sure they have enough of the tools I have described in this chapter to do their job effectively. It is a good idea for you to have them do a mock presentation using you as a prospective purchaser asking all the questions one would ask. Afterwards tell them what they did right, what they did wrong, and how they could have improved their performance; polish their techniques. Instruct your sales staff not to oversell. Most people react favorably to helpful salespeople but feel uncomfortable with pushy ones.

A few words of caution for any owner who chooses to be his or her own salesperson: Whatever you say to a prospective customer can never be withdrawn without loss of credibility. An owner can always change or clarify what an employee says without creating the same harmful effect.

The strategies that I recommend for selling homes can also be used for renting units with few variations. One or more tastefully furnished model apartments are a necessity for any large project. The customer must see for themselves the desirability and functionality of the unit. That's the best sales tool you have. If the apartment in which the customer is interested has reached a stage of completion where it is clean, finished, and painted, by all means go ahead and show it. If it's still a work in progress, don't let them see it because it is difficult for anyone to visualize a completed unit. It is also important that you have plans for each unit showing the room sizes and the rental rates for each unit on each floor. A list of the amenities that are offered should be available as a giveaway or incorporated in a visually attractive brochure.

SUMMARY

The scope of all promotions really depends on the size and nature of the product being promoted and the audience that you are looking to attract. No book can tell you whether you have overpromoted or underpromoted your project. The only guidelines a first time developer can use are those of the competitors promoting a similar product. As your experience grows so will your knowledge of what kind of promotions are best for the selling of your product and which of them proved more cost-effective than others. When in doubt—overpromote!

10

HOW TO MANAGE PROPERTY

LIKE TRUMP

Treat It as a Customer Service Business

KEY POINTS

- Develop an eye for detail.
- Treat tenants as treasured customers, not as problems.
- Be vigilant about repairs and upkeep.

AFTER COMPLETING A major building renovation or new development, Trump will often cash out and harvest the profits. In other cases, if it makes sense to buy and hold a property as a cash cow, or at least to hold on until the market improves and it can be sold or refinanced, Trump will retain ownership. Any real estate investor, even those who "flip" most of their properties, will eventually be in a situation where it makes more sense to hold. This means you must get comfortable with a subject that scares many real estate investors: managing property. In truth, it's certainly not the easiest job in the world but it's also not the hardest. Many real estate investors, especially novices, hate to be involved in managing property and suffering the headaches that go along with being a landlord. Trump typically takes the opposite approach. He has turned property management into his personal art form and made it a core element of his overall real estate investing strategy. The Trump approach to property management involves treating it as a "customer service business," and seeing tenants as valued customers. As a result, he is able to generate huge profits with his "buy and hold" or "build, sell, and manage" strategies that offer continued superb management because tenants love the amenities and the service he provides in buildings he owns or manages.

Small real estate investors can cash in on the tremendous opportunity for participation in the long-term appreciation of their properties if they employ a similar strategy. Because so many landlords are inferior, penny-pinching property managers who view their tenants only as necessary evils, problems, and headaches, investors who are smarter can become very successful by treating tenants like customers, and offering premium services at premium prices. Trump looks for ways to turn his properties into huge cash cows that are so profitable he would never contemplate selling them. Mar-a-Lago is an outstanding example of this.

INVESTING CASE STUDY

MAR-A-LAGO

Mar-a-Lago is an exquisite mansion and estate in Palm Beach, Florida, that was built in the 1920s by Marjorie Merriwether Post, the Post cereal empire heiress who later married E. F. Hutton, the financier. The mansion consists of 118 rooms with 67 bathrooms, and 62,500 square feet of floor space on 19 acres. No expense was spared to build it. For example, over 17,000 ceramic tiles used in the property were made in the sixteenth century. Marjorie Merriwether Post imported the tiles from Italy. At one time, over 300 artisans were brought in from Europe to work full time on Mar-a-Lago. During the estate's heyday as a winter home for lavish entertaining, she employed 60 people—30 working inside as butlers, maids, laundresses, cooks, and other jobs, and 30 working the outside as gardeners, handymen, chauffeurs, and security guards. Yet, only she and Dina Merrill, her daughter, lived on the property.

When Marjorie passed away, Mar-a-Lago was conveyed to a trust established by the Post family. Because of the magnificence of the building and its furnishings, the trust donated it to the federal government to be used as a museum. It was never successful as a museum because there were not enough fee-paying visitors to warrant the expenses involved in maintenance and operation. It wasn't long before the government gave it back to the trust. The trust had no viable alternative but to put the estate up for sale. However, the trustees wanted the buyer to preserve this valuable historic treasure. Donald Trump decided to bid on it and although he was not the highest bid-

Mar-a-Lago Club

der, he agreed that he would keep the premises intact and restore it to its original glory. He got the property because the trustees liked the idea that he would maintain and restore the estate and would not subdivide its 19 acres into individual parcels. As part of the sale, Trump also bought all the furnishings, which in itself, was a fabulous deal. In fact, when he decided to turn the estate into a country club, he sold some of the antique furnishings that were of museum quality for more than he paid for the entire property. Today, Mar-a-Lago, which was falling apart when Trump bought it, has been totally refurbished and is a very exclusive and beautifully restored estate and country club with a membership roster that reads like "Who's Who."

After Trump first bought the property, the expenses of operating and owning were overwhelming considering how little use Trump made of the estate. After thinking about the problem, Trump thought, "Why don't I create an elite country club and get 200 to 300 wealthy people to share the costs?" Before his idea became reality he had to fight a major battle to obtain the right to operate the facility in its present fashion. When he first bought it, city officials and the powers that be didn't like the idea of Trump, a newcomer who was not part of the old money families of Palm Beach, coming in and creating a country club on the Mar-a-Lago property. Little did they know what a tenacious adversary Trump would become.

To get approval, Trump threatened to subdivide the property which was his legal right. He never intended to do this but he used it as leverage to get what he wanted, because he knew the last thing the city wanted was a flock of new houses on this landmarked property. (This is a good example of exploiting the other side's weakness in a negotiation.) The political fight got so nasty that the West Palm Beach airport appeared to alter their takeoff and landing patterns to fly over Mar-a-Lago to weaken Trump's resolve. Trump sued the County Airport facility claiming the noise and vibrations from low flying aircraft would damage a historic federal landmark (which Mar-a-Lago was). Finally, recognizing their potential liability and the expense and embarrassment the local government would sustain, they gave Trump the approval he sought and Trump's lawsuits were terminated. Trump was now ready to implement his plan to turn Mar-a-Lago into a luxurious country club. This involved restoring the property to its former magnificence while adding improvements to make it attractive to members willing to pay $200,000 or more to join.

Trump's Mar-a-Lago Club in Palm Beach is another classic Trump example of creating "sizzle," which I discussed in Chapter 5. Trump envisioned Mar-a-Lago as a country club without the benefit of a golf course but with a host of other luxurious facilities superior to those at any other Palm Beach hotel or country club. Trump decided to make Mar-a-Lago "the place" for entertaining dinner guests, so he modernized the entire kitchen and expanded the dining areas. He created luxury suites and cottages where guests could stay for $1,000 per night. He spent millions by adding a huge cabana and pool area on the Atlantic Ocean for use by members and their guests who desired sun and surf. On the grounds, he installed a new magnificent Olympic-size swimming pool, a new tennis facility with five championship courts, and a state of the art spa and fitness center. For those who are interested in croquet, there is a championship layout on the manicured front lawn where a croquet professional is available to give lessons. Not satisfied with his installation of a huge tent that could accommodate as many as 1,000 guests, Trump recently built a new equally spacious "Trump Touch" ballroom replacing the tented facility. It's considered "the place" for weddings, parties, or charity functions. It's an absolutely spectacular facility, the ultimate in class and luxury.

It's interesting to note that many of Palm Beach's elite—people on the town boards and others who lived in the community who had vigorously opposed Trump, immediately applied to become charter members of Mar-a-Lago. They knew that a membership at Mar-a-Lago would be a symbol of prestige they had to have. They were right!

How Trump Manages Property at Mar-a-Lago

The landscaping is incredibly picturesque and painstakingly maintained. All of the public areas give the members a feeling of comfort and luxury. Although the spa and accompanying beauty salon are intimate, they are elegantly designed to display magnificent taste. The exercise area is really special—the club offers the members regular classes like hot yoga and high impact aerobics. Most country clubs or spas can't rival the facilities at Mar-a-Lago, especially considering the food service offered by a master chef and served by a well-trained staff. Throughout the season, Trump provides name entertainers such as Paul Anka, Tony Bennett, Natalie Cole, and others each weekend. The initiation fee for members is currently $250,000; food service is extra. It is a step above the finest country club you could imagine anywhere. Who but Donald Trump could picture a group of people willing to pay a quarter-of-a-million dollars to join a club primarily for a dining experience?

Mar-a-Lago not only benefits its members, it benefits Donald Trump. The initiation fee is treated as a loan to the club from members and is repayable in 30 years, thus, it's not deemed taxable but can be used to pay the cost of improvements or any other purpose Trump desires. The annual dues paid by each member and the monies received from numerous functions are more than sufficient to cover the cost of operation including real estate taxes. The club is a money-maker, and few clubs can make that claim.

DEVELOP AN EYE FOR DETAIL

Small real estate investors need to remember that the devil is in the details—be as concerned about small details as about big ones. Someone will pay more for an immaculately maintained building than they will for one with average maintenance. Mar-a-Lago is a wonderful example of Trump's keen eye for detail, which was crucial in restoring this exquisite property to its former grandeur and simultaneously catering to his new elite dues-paying clientele. Trump uses nothing but the best building materials, such as hand carved stonework, imported Italian marble, and other materials compatible with preservation of the world-class aesthetic qualities of the Mar-a-Lago estate. The club has a wine cellar capable of satisfying the palate of any connoisseur. The gourmet chef is famous for his preparation and presentation of a huge variety of dishes. The list is endless. When it comes to maintenance, Trump is truly obsessive. Trump will walk through each of his properties and personally see that all the brass is perfectly polished. If he sees something that needs repair or if an elevator is dirty, he will immediately call it to the attention of the person in charge. If an employee is not wearing a cleaned and pressed uniform, he will spot it. If a staff member doesn't answer a telephone in a timely fashion, he'll find out why.

At Mar-a-Lago, Trump is forever casting his watchful eye. If something was painted and the color is slightly off, he will insist on immediate repainting. If a newly planted tree or shrub doesn't look right to him, he will have it promptly replaced. Perhaps the best example of Trump's eye for detail can be found in the furniture throughout the estate. Because many of the original pieces were authentic antiques of museum quality, Trump decided to sell them rather than have the pieces subjected to club usage. However, before it was sold, each piece of furniture was photographed and later replaced by an exact replica.

Make people want to be in your building because you care about your property.

You can do it in the following ways:

- Make cleanliness a top priority.
- Put money into items that provide some type of service to occupants, rather than simply providing them with living quarters, for example, the superintendent should also provide some customer service like receiving and mailing packages or coordinating repairs.

- Give tenants access to a hot tub, or provide a steam unit in a stall shower, or install a granite countertop in the master bathroom.
- Install a special lighting fixture or mirror for doing makeup, or a kitchen with top of the line cabinets, or a kitchen center island, all with lots of storage space, and a well-thought-out design.
- Hire a superintendent or building manager who will be readily available and who has a pleasant customer service attitude. When you are looking for the right person to fill the bill, use the services of an employment agency, an appropriate labor union, or a local newspaper. Carefully check all references.
- Provide immediate access to a staff of experts; have phone numbers for each trade you approve, so that tenants can call them directly.
- Provide a quick response for needed repairs: If you develop a mechanism where complaints are funneled through one location and trigger an immediate response, you will generate significant goodwill with your tenants.

There are many other small details that could mean a lot to tenants—ask your tenants what they would like and they will want to stay in your property even if it means paying more rent.

TREAT TENANTS AS TREASURED CUSTOMERS, NOT AS PROBLEMS

One of the best things you can do is to hire customer-service oriented and knowledgeable property managers, who have a pleasant attitude. Many landlords treat tenants like they are the enemy. If you look for ways to delight your tenants and provide courteous, fast, service, you will have a great advantage over your competition. One method Trump employs in his office buildings is access to a web site called

"Workspeed." If a tenant has a complaint of any kind, such as an electrical malfunction, he logs onto Workspeed and furnishes details of the nature and location of the problem. This information is immediately sent by Workspeed to the person responsible for electrical maintenance. That person logs in the time the complaint was received, who will respond, and when it will be corrected. All of this information also goes to the building office enabling it to monitor the problem and the efficiency of the repair crew. This procedure bypasses busy telephones in the building office, prevents a repair person from saying I never got the complaint, and eliminates a claim by an irate tenant saying, "I've called five times and haven't gotten any response."

The following anecdote portrays the kind of customer service that real estate investors can learn from. Just recently, I was about to enter a particular non-Trump casino, and there was a security guard sitting at the podium perhaps eight feet from the entry doors, which had to be opened manually. She saw me coming, got up from her chair, greeted me with a friendly smile and a good morning sir, and walked over to the entryway to open the door for me. When I entered the casino, it looked very clean and well-maintained. The result was that it made me feel like someone special. Now whether she did this courteous act on her own, or she was trained in customer service I don't know. What I do know is that three months earlier when I entered the same casino precisely at the same entryway, the security guard sitting at the same podium never even looked up and acknowledged me. The little extra effort by a courteous security guard made a very positive impression on me. Now if you owned this property, wouldn't you want all your employees to make this kind of impression on customers?

If there are several casinos all bunched together in the same spot, and each one essentially offers the same types of gambling games, most players will prefer the casino that makes its customers feel special.

How You Can Give Great Service to a Small Rental Property

One easy solution to property management is for you, the owner, to live in one of the units. That way you can ensure that the building and grounds are kept clean and in impeccable condition. If you're mechanically inclined, you can promptly repair and maintain most things that need fixing.

In the other scenario, you own a four-unit building but do not live in it. It would be desirable to have someone living on-site being responsible for lost keys, showing vacancies, doing minor repairs, and performing a host of other services. Make one of your best tenants responsible for overseeing the property and give them a rent reduction as an inducement. For repair work and landscaping, you are better off paying an outsider. It's important that tenants have immediate access to someone when they need assistance, like a super or a handyman. At a minimum, you need someone on the property who will call you, the owner, when a situation arises needing your attention.

TIP on Rent Collection

Never allow your resident manager or superintendent to accept cash for rent or any other reason. Only in emergencies should you, and only you, ever accept cash. Your on-site managers can be allowed to accept checks or money orders. This helps to eliminate the opportunity of theft or embezzlement of the owner's income or arguments as to what happened to cash or the amount delivered.

BE VIGILANT ABOUT REPAIRS AND UPKEEP

Throughout this book, I've talked about the ways Trump gets premium prices for his properties by offering impressive luxuries people aren't used to seeing. He will only use the finest marble, and each piece has to match. He will only use mirrored steel and it has to be perfect. It's one thing to use these materials; it's another to keep them in pristine condition.

Trump's philosophy on repairs and maintenance is unwavering: Everything must be constantly maintained by skilled personnel. What other building owners and property managers do is not good enough for Trump. The windows must be cleaned every few weeks; not just four times a year like other properties. Elevator carpets are vacuumed three times a day, not once a week. Uniforms have to be clean and pressed and fit properly. (By the way, the uniforms in Trump buildings are designed with more flourish and distinction than typical uniforms.) If you go into any Trump building, you will notice that the marble floors are always highly polished and all glass is spotless. A Trump rule for his properties is, "Don't wait until it's broken to fix it, fix it before it breaks."

This level of vigilance concerning service, maintenance, and repairs is one of the reasons Trump International Hotel in New York City, which has always had a Five-Star rating, was recently voted the best hotel in New York City by *Travel & Leisure* magazine. This property is not even branded with one of the big-name hotel chains, such as The Four Seasons, Hyatt, or Ritz Carlton. Even without major name recognition, it was rated the number one hotel in New York City. Capitalizing on Trump's reputation for quality and service, it also charges the highest rates of any hotel in New York City—which guests willingly pay.

SUMMARY

People have a tendency to think that just because something is small it doesn't require much attention. The fact is that size has nothing to do with it. The more you are personally involved in the details of property ownership, the more people will recognize your building as the one they want to be in because you are an owner who cares. It's exactly what I've been stressing when I discuss Trump buildings, like Mar-a-Lago. It's service, service, service. It's hiring courteous, knowledgeable, and friendly people. It's insisting on total cleanliness. It's putting money into servicing the occupants and not just the building. You have to concentrate on being different or exclusive. Of course, you don't want to be so radical that your property becomes unappealing to the market you're targeting. It must be in good taste and functional, which in turn will make it desirable. For instance, the availability of a concierge not located in the building, but at least accessible to occupants would be a great added service. Another example could be a building newsletter, which many tenants could find informative. Again, it's being different or exclusive from what others are doing. To the extent a clever and creative small investor can find ways to service the occupants and make their building better than the competition, it will show up in increased profits. People will pay more if they get more. It's as simple as that.

11

HOLDING STRATEGIES AND EXIT STRATEGIES

KEY POINTS

- Plan several possible ownership timelines.
- Holding strategies.
- Exit strategies.

W ITH THE EXCEPTION of condominium units, Donald Trump, like most savvy real estate investors, seldom sells his real estate investments that are good income producers. If he sells any of his real estate holdings, he would have to reinvest the proceeds in something, and what better place to have your money than in a good solid chunk of mother earth. As an investor in real estate, you should realize that it's very difficult, not to mention very time consuming, to find another good real estate investment where you can park sale proceeds.

With that in mind, the following are key principles that will help you to determine whether or not to sell a particular real estate investment, along with several real estate holding or exit strategies for your consideration.

PLAN SEVERAL POSSIBLE OWNERSHIP TIMELINES

Trump always tries to estimate when his properties are likely to reach their maximum value to help him decide how long to hold on to a property or when to offer it for sale. Small investors should create several possible timelines for ownership, including when you might want to sell, and what you expect to gain or lose, depending on how long you hold the property.

Fix and Flip

The shortest holding timeline is the "fix-and-flip" strategy. This entails purchasing the property, building on it or renovating it, and then selling it for a profit. Trump often uses this strategy but without selling the whole building. For example, Trump will "flip" enough residential condo units in a building he has just completed to pay for the construction costs of the property and recoup his initial investment. However, if it's a good income-producing property, he will also keep some kind of an ownership interest and enjoy the income it produces.

Keep in mind that when you sell, it is not essential to sell the property for all cash. Consider selling it on an installment basis under a land contract or take back a purchase money mortgage at a favorable rate of interest and earn profit for a longer term. When Trump bought the GM Building in New York City, it was the biggest "fixer-upper" I ever saw. This deal is discussed in detail in Chapter 6. He spent millions of dollars creating a new plaza area; a magnificent lobby; and state of the art elevators, electrical, HVAC, and other building systems. The completion of the improvements generated higher rental rates, which increased the building's value immensely. After only a few years of ownership, the increased rents enabled the building to be sold at a huge profit.

These are things to consider when you create timelines:

1. Do I think my ownership of this project is short term (five years or less), or long term?
2. Do I want to pass ownership of this real estate to my heirs?
3. Do I intend to sell it without developing it (such as property bought for land banking)?
4. Do I intend to develop it and then sell it?
5. Can I afford to hold on to the property if the real estate market goes south for a few years and my rental income suffers?
6. When am I going to be required to make expensive capital improvements?
7. Does the property throw off a good income?

Short Term or Long Term?

The first thing you have to do is to take into account the nature of the investment. If, for example, you're investing in a stable residential location, you want to buy it and hold on to it. That's a long-term investment since in all likelihood it will always do well and throw off a steady income that will keep up with any inflation that may occur. If, on the other hand, you're buying something that has a questionable life cycle, such as a strip mall without long-term leases or large anchor tenants, I would view that as a short-term investment, and would try to sell it quickly if vacancies are likely to occur and adequate replacements might be problematical. If you choose to invest in a retail or commercial or industrial property with a long-term lease with a financially stable tenant, think long term.

Real Estate Cycles

Any real estate investor whether large or small must acknowledge the fact that the real estate market runs in cycles that have unpredictable timing and duration. When the interest rates for mortgages are high, the sale of homes or apartment units will drop. Increases in the rate of unemployment or a recession will also produce negative effects.

There are some aspects of real estate I think you can bank on. One is that the cost of construction will rise as time goes on. Another is that there is a limited supply of real estate for any worthwhile use. Although it is difficult to predict any real estate cycle with a reasonable degree of accuracy, there are many sources that track trends and report their findings. Government sources are the least reliable because they are not specific as to area. Reports created by local reputable real estate brokers, local banks, or financial institutions are a far better source to rely on. The best research advice I can give to any real estate investor is to gather as much information as you can from as many sources as you can and reach your own informed conclusion as to market trends.

Selling When the Market Is Hot

A classic example of timing a sale was demonstrated by Leonard Kandell who made his fortune by constructing and leasing residential apartment buildings in New York City. Traditionally, he was a long-term holder. However, when the idea of converting apartment buildings into cooperative apartments became red hot, there were any number of avid buyers scrambling to buy residential rental buildings with the objective of converting them into co-op apartments, so the units could be sold individually for high prices. The problem faced by any owner wishing to convert a building to cooperative ownership was getting 15 percent of the renters in the building to agree to buy their apartments. That was a legal requirement in the State of New York before the owner was permitted to declare his cooperative plan effective. That's where extensive negotiation came in. If you didn't get 15 percent, you couldn't declare the co-op plan effective and there was a waiting period before you could try again. So getting 15 percent of tenants to buy often involved complex negotiations relating to the price they would be willing to pay for their apartments and what they wanted the owner to do for them to induce them to become buyers. Once the co-op plan was effective, eviction proceedings were possible to permit the owner to get possession of the remaining units and sell them to new buyers. Agreeing to exorbitant payoffs to some tenants became the norm.

Kandell owned many apartment buildings and he regarded his tenants as family. When I asked him why he didn't cash in on the conversion boom he said, "I don't want to fight with my tenants over turning their building into a co-op. Let someone else have the headaches and reap the rewards. Since the market for apartment buildings that are ripe for conversion to co-ops is hot, I will sell them at a premium to people who want to convert them and I'll take the money to buy land in a good location that has a long-term ground lease."

Kandell made a conscious decision to give up the income that he had from apartment rentals, sell the buildings at high prices because of the particular demand that existed at that time, and turn the money into a safe, gilt edge, and passive investment in ground leases. Taking advantage of favorable tax treatment, he swapped a building that could go co-op for a ground lease that was owned by my old client, Sol Goldman. The land Goldman swapped was under a major office structure, known as the Newsweek building on Madison Avenue. The rate of return was lower than Kandell earned from the apartment building but it was a rock-solid investment that would ultimately appreciate in value. By repeating this investment technique, Kandell amassed a considerable fortune that he left for his heirs without the headaches connected with active ownership and operation of apartment buildings. I learned later that some of the co-op conversions of Kandell buildings never got off the ground primarily because of fights with tenants that ended up in the courts. Kandell took advantage of an opportunity to cash in when the time was ripe and changed his investment strategy to a more conservative one. Whenever the market is hot for the type of property you own, you should consider selling and reaping large profits, then putting the money into another type of real estate for which the demand, and the price, is not so high.

HOLDING STRATEGIES

The following are examples of several strategies that successful realty investors utilize. Some of the strategies are short term and some are long term.

Land Banking

This strategy is long-term in nature, because you're investing in a property that you intend to hold, and then either develop it some time in the future or sell it to someone else who will. For example, you could buy land and use it as a parking lot with the intention of building an office building at some time in the future, when demand for office space is greater.

Another example of land banking would be building relatively low-cost storage rental units on a site that you feel will be very strategic at some future time. Meanwhile, you rent out the storage units with the intention of someday tearing the units down and building something more profitable on the site, such as a retail store or a fast-food operation. Land banking could consist of buying a vacant lot or a building in the path of future development then selling it when the time is right.

I came across a classic example of land banking quite by accident. My wife was talking to a friend of hers who mentioned that her husband, Jerry, was offered almost $5 million to give up his lease on a bar and grill on 6th Avenue in New York City. My wife didn't think she got the story straight and asked me to talk to Jerry and find out the details. Jerry confirmed to me that he was negotiating with a Rockefeller affiliate to sell the lease on his bar and grill for somewhere around $5 million, but he thought that it sounded fishy and wasn't sure it was a serious offer, because the price was so high. When he told me the location of his bar I knew it was in a strategic location where a new high-rise office building was contemplated. I told Jerry, "It's entirely possible this is a legitimate offer and if you decide to accept the lease buyout you need a good real estate lawyer and a good tax accountant. I'm not looking for work but if you need me I'm available as the lawyer." It was a Friday and he told me he was going to Las Vegas over the weekend and he'd think it over. Saturday night I got a call from Jerry asking me to be his lawyer on the deal. I agreed and asked him, "Jerry, why couldn't you wait until you came back to New York? Why did you call me on a Saturday night?" His answer was, "When I flew out last night I was sitting beside a man who happened to mention that he was a big real estate operator. I told him my whole story and he said there's only one lawyer you should use, George Ross, he's my lawyer but he's probably too busy to handle your matter. So I decided I better call you right away."

I got Jerry his $5 million and he was so excited he thought he had discovered an untapped world of real estate opportunity. He said he was thinking of buying property in another area he perceived as a strategic location and go into land banking as a business. I warned him, "Jerry, what happened to you is a fluke. Don't think it will happen again. I strongly suggest that you put the money into something you know." A short time later he asked me what I thought of a particular property he was contemplating buying for land banking. I told him, "Jerry, forget it, I know that block. Sol Goldman has it locked up with the piece next door and you'll die holding the piece you're contemplating buying." He didn't like my comment so he hired another lawyer and bought the parcel I warned him about. In three years, he managed to blow the entire $5 million. Be forewarned: Land banking is not for the timid or those with limited resources. Staying power is a prerequisite.

Renting with a Buy Option

Renting houses or apartments has always been a great way for realty investors to show a good return on their investment. However, when it comes to renting houses to tenants, there's another potential method one can use to earn an even greater return. You can do it by giving a tenant an option to buy the house; if they choose to buy, you will agree to apply a portion of the rent toward a specified purchase price. For example, say you rent a house for $950 per month and you give the tenant the option to buy it within a specified time. You agree that if the tenant exercises the option to buy, you will allow

$200 per month to be applied toward the purchase price. If the tenant stays for a period of years he or she will have an incentive to buy rather than leave and lose the opportunity.

Conversions

Sometime a piece of real estate requires a change of use to achieve a greater value. If you have a residential building that isn't doing well and the zoning permits the change to office use, check it out. If it's cost-effective based on the cost of the conversion and the increased income from office rents (which are often twice residential rents), you should give it serious consideration. The reverse can also be true especially if you're converting to condominiums or co-ops. The sale of condo units could bail you out of a poor investment. Sometimes, when circumstances warrant it, municipalities grant incentives to induce owners to convert their buildings to other uses. Finding out if there are any incentives and their value could make a difference in your decision.

The Ultimate Holding Strategy—Bringing in a "Watchdog"

Once again I must use Leonard Kandell as a prime example of brilliant foresight and real estate savvy. Kandell owned land on Central Park South in New York City under a ground lease owned by the operator of a Ritz Carlton Hotel. It was a valuable piece of land in a very strategic spot with a major hotel on it under a lease which had approximately 50 years left to run. The hotel was run by an operator named John Coleman, but Kandell owned the land. Kandell found Coleman an extremely difficult man to deal with. He was a source of constant trouble: perpetually late in paying rent, taxes, and negligent in carrying insurance. Kandell did not like the aggravation of dealing with difficult people and so had absolutely no regard for him as a tenant. He considered Coleman untrustworthy.

With a view toward solving his problem, Kandell asked me if I thought it would be okay if he asked Donald Trump to be his watchdog on this particular piece of property. Now it is very unusual to ask someone to be a guardian of a real estate interest and I had never seen it employed where the person to be the protector was not a family member but merely a business acquaintance. The determining factor in Kandell's mind was his concern that Coleman would be too tough for his children and grandchildren to handle when they inherited the property, and he didn't savor the idea that they would eventually have to deal with such a difficult man. Instead, he reasoned, "I'm going to use Donald Trump as a protective shield and let Coleman deal with Donald Trump. Trump will know how to handle someone like Coleman." Kandell had the confidence that Donald Trump would protect the valuable asset for him and his family.

Kandell gave Trump an overriding lease which locked in behind the Coleman lease and had a longer term. If the Coleman lease was terminated or expired, Trump's lease became effective. Now Coleman would have to deal with Trump when it came to any issue under his lease. Over the first four years, Trump got nothing for riding herd on Coleman but his being in the picture intimidated Coleman who sold his lease to another hotel operator. The land eventually came up for reappraisal to determine a new and higher rent. Pursuant to Trump's overriding lease he was obligated to negotiate the reappraisal and would be entitled to retain 15 percent of any increase in rent. When the time for reappraisal occurred I, as Trump's representative, dealt with Coleman's successor. I negotiated the new rent and was able to get a hefty increase, which continued until 2004 when as a result of changed circumstances, the lease was renegotiated.

Leonard S. Kandell died in 1991 at the age of 85. His ground lease has since passed through three hotel operators, and each time I was involved as the overseer on behalf of Trump. I supervised the collection of rents, payment of taxes, and made sure that the tenant performed all of its obligations contained in the lease.

Recently, the current leaseholder, a hotel chain, wanted to sell its leasehold, but the remaining term of the lease was too short (approximately 50 years) to attract an operator willing to pay the asking price. They decided to put the lease out for bids. The highest bid came from a developer who intended to convert the building from a hotel to a luxury cooperative residential building. The bid was conditioned on completion of a successful renegotiation of the ground lease, extending the term, permitting co-op ownership, and eliminating Trump's leasehold position. After extensive negotiations the revision of the lease was agreed on and the lease was assigned to the developer. As a result of this deal, Trump received a big chunk of money for giving up his position, and he still receives 15 percent of the increased ground lease rent. The Kandell family also got a substantial amount of money for revamping the ground lease plus 85 percent of the increase in rent.

Trump is still obligated to oversee the tenant's performance under the ground lease on behalf of Kandell's heirs. If Leonard Kandell were alive today, I think he would still be happy with the decision he made. This was Kandell's long-term holding strategy that would protect his family forever. During his lifetime and even in contemplation of death, he had respect for and trust in Donald Trump, highly unusual because they were on opposite sides of the negotiation table throughout his career.

EXIT STRATEGIES

Sell property when interest rates are low but indications are that they're going up.

When the cost of borrowing money is cheap you can get a better price for your real estate because the leverage is better. Leverage is the difference between the rate of return on a "free and clear" basis and the rate of return on invested capital. For example, suppose you are buying a small office building for $10 million and the annual cash flow is $1 million. That's a 10 percent return on a free and clear basis. Now instead of buying the property for all cash, assume you take out a mortgage of $8 million (80 percent of the purchase price) at an annual interest rate of 7 percent. The annual cost of the mortgage portion of the investment is $560,000. The annual return on your $2 million investment is $440,000 or 22 percent on your cash. That's how fortunes are built.

There is usually a high demand for real estate when the stock market and the bond market show low returns. It is also true when the rate of exchange of the dollar for foreign currencies is low because foreign investors see bargains in the making. When the rate of inflation starts to rise dramatically buyers will often flock to real estate because increase in real estate prices and rents seem to rise in line with the rate of inflation.

If you have a piece of property in an area that is deteriorating as indicated by "for sale" or "for rent" signs or by increased boarded up or vacant stores or buildings and you have no solid information as to when this cycle will change—get out! Take a loss, if you have to, but get out! If interest rates are rising and you have a mortgage, which will be coming due shortly, sell, preferably to an investor that has lots of ready cash, but sell!

If you own a building which is going to be adversely affected by a change in traffic patterns or new interstates or highways, sell as soon as you have reason to believe that any of those items will become a reality. If you have a building that you believe will be adversely affected by some new construction in the area, that's also a time to sell. This is especially true if you have a property with retail stores and new, larger or serious competition is on the way.

You should consider selling real estate when you encounter obstacles to the project, such as denial of zoning or approvals and the projected critical path of your project is no longer feasible. You should also consider selling if key relationships or people you rely on drastically change or leave the picture.

Exit Strategy for Partnership Interests

Partnerships or joint ventures are excellent vehicles for blending diverse investing interests into a cohesive business entity. One partner may put in nothing but money, another may put in both money and expertise, a third may contribute land. The documentation binding them together requires careful planning, this is particularly true when they are not equal partners with equal control.

It is likely at some point in time that the desires of various partners may not be the same. One may want to sell the property and another may not. The solution is a divorce mechanism that is fair and equitable. A typical provision often used in two-party partnerships is what is commonly called the "shotgun clause." The clause provides that if either party wants to sell, he contacts the other party and says, "I want you to buy me out and here's what I want for my interest." The other party either elects to accept the offer or can elect to sell his share to the other party for the same amount of money properly adjusted for varying percentage interests. While this provision seems fair, it has many potential pitfalls. The major one exists when the parties are not financial equals. The partner with limited funds is at a distinct disadvantage. Another disadvantage is the timing may not be right for a buyout if there are more cash calls imminent that cannot be met.

Another apparent solution is to permit a partner to sell his interest in the partnership after first offering it to the other partners. This concept is not really an equitable solution for anyone. Who is willing to pay full value for a partial interest in a partnership with partners they don't know? Certainly the remaining partners don't want to deal with a stranger who suddenly becomes their partner. If someone buys that interest at a highly discounted price, he may be doing so solely for the purpose of tormenting the other partners to a point where they, too, will sell their interests at a bargain price just to buy peace.

A better approach and one that is fair and equitable for all partners goes like this: Partner A wants out. He obtains a bona fide offer for the entire property that he is willing to accept. He notifies all other partners of his intention to sell and they have two options. One, they can elect to buy the share of Partner A and pay him what he would have received if the sale were made or two, they must join in the sale. This completely eliminates any monetary discount for a minority interest and the possibility that remaing partners will have to deal with a stranger.

SUMMARY

Well-located real estate has supreme value because of its finite supply. No one's making any more land. And for that reason alone, real estate improved with the kind of creativity and savvy that Trump puts into his real estate investments will always be in demand and will always increase in value. The strategies in this book have made billions for Trump and can help you make a large or small fortune in the world of real estate.

INDEX

INDEX

INDEX